How to Deal With Narcissists

Why They're Evil, How They Think, and
Strategies and Techniques to Take Control

Michael Trust

Federalist Publications
Macclenny, Florida

Published by Federalist Publications, Macclenny, Florida

Please direct all communications to :
Author@AnonymousConservative.com

www.anonymousconservative.com

Printed in the United States of America
ISBN-13 : 978-0-9829479-6-8 (Cloth Hardcover, Jacketed)
ISBN-13 : 978-0-9829479-7-5 (Softcover)
ISBN-13 : 978-0-9829479-8-2 (Amazon Kindle)

Library of Congress Control Number: 2014942759

Library of Congress Subject Headings:

Psychology.
Psychology and religion.
Good and evil -- Psychological aspects.
Psychopathology.
Religion and Psychology.
Social problems -- United States.

"A moderately bad man knows he is not very good: a thoroughly bad man thinks he's alright."

- C.S. Lewis

Table of Contents

Why Link Narcissists and Political Leftists?

Dr. M Scott Peck wrote in *People of the Lie*, that evil was, "*The exercise of political power – that is, the imposition of one's will upon others by overt or covert coercion, in order to avoid... spiritual growth,*" and that evil was often rooted in narcissism. Narcissists expect everyone else to sacrifice and stifle their own accomplishments and ability, so that the narcissist's insecurity will not bother them as much. You see this with leftism everywhere. Where others are rich, the leftist expects to be allowed to take their wealth through government fiat, so they won't be so rich in comparison to the leftist. Where others can defend their families, the leftist expects them to weaken themselves by surrendering their weapons, so the leftist will not feel so inferior and impotent in that regard. The leftist is unable to confront a reality where they are not dominant and superior, so they seek to use government to force others to lessen themselves. Rather than focus on their own growth and development of their own self-sufficiency, the leftist seeks to have government steal the accomplishments, and suppress the self-sufficiency of others, on their behalf.

Some have said I shouldn't politicize this work, however politicization does three things, which are all of benefit, in my opinion.

First, I believe in individual freedom ardently, and believe the leftist's urges to enlarge government will hand ever more power to ever fewer elites. As this occurs, the resultant corruption will stifle the opportunities for anyone to accomplish anything, and that is bad for individual freedom as well as for America. Leftists are not my people, and it is my opinion that any obstacle which hampers their lives, helps freedom. So it is my hope that politicizing this work will deprive leftists of any benefits from it. If the social narcissists can take up the time of the political narcissists, those are all fewer narcissists occupying the lives of the good people.

Second, I believe firmly that political leftism is a form of Narcissistic Personality Disorder, especially in the more ardent of leftist ideologues. If you are a Leftist, merely by expressing your big-government, ideological beliefs, you betray a personal worldview in which you believe yourself to be superior to individual citizens, you believe those citizens need your Leftist dictates forced upon them in order to live their lives "correctly," and anyone who opposes this assertion of your superiority, and the righteousness of your total domination of their lives, is somehow evil. If that isn't the narcissist's worldview, I don't know what is. Say what you will of small government Conservatives and Libertarians – they do not seek to exert their will on others through governmental force. In neutering government, they deem no specific man's judgment, let alone their personal judgment, as necessary for the masses of individuals to lead noble, moral lives. Since narcissists and leftists are all the same, in elucidating the weaknesses of the narcissist, this work will also provide strategies to attack the weaknesses of leftists, and readers interested in freedom should be aware of that. That is best accomplished by pointing the similarities out, and that can only be done by politicizing this work.

Third, it is my hope that political leftists who read this will perhaps question, why exactly are they supporting "taxes on the rich," as opposed to simply contributing more to charity themselves, mentoring an impoverished child themselves, or even supporting a more general increase in welfare spending, funded by all citizens equally? Why do they not demand anything of the poor in return for the welfare? Why do they try to disarm law-abiding citizens, when all of the relevant science shows, law-abiding citizens who have guns actually deter criminal attacks? Their policies are, without any doubt, an attack on the happy and successful, cloaked in false motives that are designed to shield them from any well-justified counter-attack.

This distaste for the happiness of others is why they try to keep citizens out of wilderness areas, oppress successful businesses with ever more burdensome regulatory and taxation schemes, oppose the traditional family structure (replacing it with bizarrely grotesque family structures almost guaranteed to produce dysfunction and unhappiness in the unfortunate children raised therein), lobby on behalf of the interests of those who would kill Americans, and grow an ever larger government whose only purpose becomes not the protection of citizens, not the protection of freedom, but rather the application of force, to crush those who strive to succeed and enjoy happiness. It is all envy and cowardice, mixed with a selfish inability to see things from the perspective of someone who only wishes to give everyone freedom from the mob's demands. It is all blind to the agency of others, which is the single most noxious aspect of the narcissistic personality.

By comparison to the Tea Party, whose sole goal is the diminution of the size and scope of government, the diminution of its interference in people's lives, and it's emphasis on personal freedom from outside oppression, the nature of Liberal evil should be clear, as should its relationship to Narcissistic Personality Disorder. The leftist political ideology is, *"The exercise of political power – that is, the imposition of one's will upon others by overt or covert coercion, in order to avoid... spiritual growth."*

Politicizing this robs any leftist of the ability to benefit from this work, and there is much benefit to be gained herein. There is no point in removing any enemy the leftist faces, for they will not seek happiness once their enemy is gone. They will only redouble their efforts to make everyone else as miserable as they are.

Prologue

Years ago I happened on the description of narcissists from the DSM IV in an article on Narcissistic Personality Disorder. I read the technical description and processed it, but never drew from the article what the narcissist really was, or why that psychology was significantly different from that of a normal person. The article described traits like shallowness and grandiosity and drew a picture of a person who thought they were great, but didn't care about others. The article then likened various politicians to narcissists, describing examples of each one's narcissistic traits, such as sensitivity to criticism, shallowness, and self-aggrandizement.

If you are reading this, you are aware that such a description is nowhere near sufficient to describe, to the uninitiated, what the narcissist is, or the deleterious effects that they can have on someone else's life. Even worse, it vastly undervalues the dangers of the narcissist, while completely failing to describe how interesting their psychology really is. I came away from the article with the view of a narcissist as an uninteresting, if vaguely amusing tool, awed by his own imaginary greatness, and oblivious to the needs and desires of those around him.

Worse, the article went on to say that we all have narcissistic traits, so the narcissist exhibits many traits that we all have, only in exaggerated form. Of course narcissism is a scale, and not all of it is black or white. But the narcissists this book will describe are very different from you or me. To imply that they exhibit traits similar to our own is to grossly mislead victims who desperately need to understand that the narcissist is something completely different from anything they have encountered before.

Narcissists are extraordinarily dangerous, but they are also fascinating, if you know how to look at them. Most importantly, you must realize that they are not passively drawn to urges that you exhibit mildly, like self-absorption (personal self-interest, in extreme form) or grandiosity (self-esteem, in extreme form), and they don't do harm merely because they don't think about you.

The narcissists we will describe here are dangerous because rather than be drawn towards a harmless behavior that you exhibit, by an urge to do it, they are driven, without choice, to extraordinarily harmful behaviors that you would never consider, by an agonizing pain in their mind which will torment them wildly, if they do not cede to its malicious whim. Sadly, this pain in their mind will give them no choice but to harm others around them, often illogically.

Everything else about them, the grandiosity, the need for attention, the seeming obliviousness to those around them, the refusal to accept criticism – these traits are all merely window dressing - adaptations designed to shield them from this deeper, fundamental, horrific pain which is the real, underlying motive force behind their disorder. Every trait of the narcissist is an attempt to short circuit this fundamental pain, before it can rend their psyche. Understand that single painful motive force, and you can understand everything about the narcissist – and how totally different from you they are.

I never grasped what the narcissist was until I realized two things. First, I was being numbed mentally from the noxious nature of my interactions with one. Literally, he was so noxious that my brain was turning off and tuning out around him. Second, I simultaneously realized he was grossly detached from reality. Once I realized something was really wrong with him, I began to examine him closer, and suddenly I saw everything that my mental numbness had been shielding me from – and it was shocking.

If you are reading this, you probably have a close familiarity with one of these characters. But some of you may be reading this just out of curiosity, or you may still be numb to the horror of your life with one, and thus don't know you are in contact with one. So for a moment, I would like to address those readers who don't even know they have a problem.

Since I began writing about this, I have heard from every manner of person, experiencing every manner of horror. Many had spent decades, blind to the evil under their nose, and enduring the awfulness – for loyalty, for family, for image, or simply because they didn't realize that all of the problems they were enduring were due to the mentally ill idiot right in front of them.

As an example, there is the story of the woman with Chronic Fatigue Syndrome. For years, she couldn't make it out of her bed, so she stayed there day after day. Her stomach was always a knot of sickness, her joints were all inflamed, she was weak beyond imagination, and she felt as if the food she was eating was poisoning her. She was sick and fatigued all of the time. Suddenly, she had to return to her parents for a family emergency, and her husband couldn't leave work to join her. In a few days, she was fully cured. She returned home, and became sick again. Thinking that her house might have been emitting something which was sickening her, she went to her parents with her husband, and no relief was found. She eventually figured out that it was her husband, divorced him, and was fully cured. Had he been poisoning her for decades? Was his personality so noxious she got physically sick around him? Nobody knows, and she didn't care. She got free, and became happy and healthy.

She lost decades thinking that she was irredeemably physically ill, attributing her problems to anything other than the real cause, and would probably still be ill, had fate not drawn her away, and opened her eyes. Moreover, nobody could have told her it was her husband – she would never have believed such awful physical symptoms could have been inflicted upon her by someone who she was loyal to. Nor could she believe that even if selfish, her husband would have thrown away her loyalty, just to hurt her, of all people – a loyal partner who only wished him well.

Of course, as a narcissist, her husband probably felt that he had no choice. Were she not sick and miserable, she might have succeeded wildly in life, and even eventually left him, for a better man. To his brain, that panic would have been all that he could focus on, and it would have been intolerable. So by making her sick and keeping her miserable, it assuaged his mental agony, and gave him the relaxation of a feeling of control, which was all that mattered in his NPD-afflicted mind. That it ultimately made her leave, was not on his radar, so it never had any effect on his mental calculations, while any image of her loyalty was totally eclipsed by his panic and fear. You see why you can't apply logic to the decisions of a narcissist. Focused only on the moment in front of them, and overwhelmed by the panic it creates, they think differently.

So if you are reading this for curiosity, while wracked with some unsolvable problems in your life, do a quick assessment of those around you. Does anyone scream a lot? Freak out periodically? Do they wear a weird, anguished expression that prevents them from making a normal blank expression on their face? Do they start fights at the dinner table reliably? Have troubled relationships with other members of their family? Have a long and troubled work history? Have few or no close friends that they talk with regularly? Could your problems have any relation to any of the people around you, even just tangentially? The narcissist is a master of hiding their involvement, and as anyone who deals with their victims can assert, mysterious illnesses that doctors have great trouble diagnosing can easily be the narcissist's doing.

For those who have suffered, if you have known a narcissist and escaped, this book is rich in new material. However, you might benefit even more from seeking professional help. This book will enhance your understanding of your enemy, but it will not repair any neural miswirings that they may have created in you. If you've dealt closely with a narcissist, you know it can be a wild, mind-bending ride. This book is in no way a substitute for competent psychological counseling, custom-tailored to make sure all the mind-bending you endured, while rubbed up against the defective who brought you here, is fixed and repaired so you can once again enjoy the world fully.

People have written me, seeking help, and found small pieces of information I had offered could change how their brain worked – radically. After reading these ideas, panic attacks they suffered were suddenly seen a different way, as they happened. Without even knowing why, they focused more on the new idea than the panic inducing stimulus, and the attacks regressed in severity dramatically.

This book may contain such a nugget or two. Something minor that you do might get changed, and greatly increase the happiness of your life. You might just see your past in a different light, and feel like it wasn't so bad. These things can affect how you go forward.

A competent professional who specializes in narcissists, however, can give you a torrent of such minor adjustments to how your brain works, and the thoughts which pass through it. It is what they have trained to do, and they may have seen thousands of cases similar to yours. It doesn't take drugs, or surgery – just a small amount of time to lay out any issues you have, and listen to the professional offer different ways to think about it, or different parts of it to focus upon. For a few hours of your time, you might find your happiness in this world radically increased.

Professionals offer an additional advantage. They can give you insights into how your narcissist thinks. Different narcissists have subtle nuances which differ between them, and these create different weaknesses in them. Laying out your case to a competent professional can allow you to acquire a detailed profile of your own narcissist, and a keen understanding of exactly how they think, what they might do in the future, and how to operate around them.

This work is the product of a close study of under ten narcissists I have happened across, and a more distant observation of several more. It is far from comprehensive, or complete. If you have a problem of sufficient severity, please see a professional, give them all your information, and ask for their help. They will be happy to provide it. Intelligence is vital to all warfare.

Finally, much of this book will be about the power within subtlety, and that is something which worries me. It will discuss how minor actions can yield results you would never believe, unless you saw them firsthand. I liken some of what it describes to hypnosis, though that is probably a mild overstatement. However, it is a useful analogy, in that if someone described hypnosis to you, and you had never heard of it, would you have believed it? This book will contain something similar – a way to exercise a fair amount of force on the cognition of narcissists, merely with words.

I worry when I write these things, because years ago I would never have believed them myself. I remember well the intellectual inertia of my inexperience in this area. I was in a race to accumulate as much knowledge about anything, as quickly as possible. As a result, if something didn't immediately comport with my raw, un-nuanced perceptions, I was quick to disregard it, and move on in search of the next easy insight or quick breakthrough.

I ask you to avoid this, and look for the wisdom here – especially if you are dealing with a narcissist. It will save you decades in your pursuit of knowledge, and give you an all important insight into the most important of psychologies – those so damaged and aberrant that you could not possibly believe that they would think as they do. I will do my best to help you overcome your inertia with early, slow, forceful insights designed to take you from stasis to movement in this area. I only ask that you do your best to not fight against them, and commit what you read here to memory. If you can do that, I can almost guarantee that it will serve you well some day. Everyone will deal with a narcissist at some point in their life.

One reader, after reading some earlier work in this vein, wrote of it to others;

"First read yields: "this stuff is crazy".

Second read yields: "this guy is smart, but the content is still crazy"

Third read yields: "Ok I need to try these techniques"

End result conclusion: "This is genius."

If you try the techniques described herein, you will find the same thing, even if at first glance they seem silly.

Unlike the earlier related collaborative work, *The Evolutionary Psychology Behind Politics[1]*, this work will not waste time on scientifically substantiating every observation it makes. Indeed, unlike that earlier work, much within here is anecdotal, and not to be found in other literature of which I am aware. However, this work did not arise out of thin air. It was earned through awful experiences with the most noxious of psychologies, combined with an unwavering drive to stare into the horrible abyss, all in the hope that truths would emerge and reveal themselves, and some of it might be of benefit.

As you read this, set aside your own psychology. Do not skeptically ask if any of this would apply to you. The psychologies we describe are those so bizarre, that you cannot easily imagine how they think. These are the individuals who actually enjoy the suffering of good people who helped them, and feel even more giddy if they can get their victim to continue to service them, even as they betray them. They are the individuals who, given a chance to enjoy life themselves, are willing to forgo all personal enjoyment, just so they may make others as miserable as themselves. They are even the individuals who look down on baffled victims who are about to be killed - victims who even at the moment of their death, are probably more confused than scared. These people are out there, and they are far more common than you would think. The most fundamental element of their camouflage is the decency of the decent people of the world – people who can not believe that anyone could think in such a bizarre fashion - let alone that their numbers might be legion, and the person they are loyal to might be one.

This work will begin where the narcissist began, examining an anecdotal case from my experience which may explain how some of these individuals first came into being, and how their brain became broken. Once you understand where the narcissist comes from, the work

---

1 Occasionally made available for free, in Kindle form, at
   http://www.anonymousconservative.com

will progress to where they end up, and examine all the techniques they use, to both control their own perceptions, and manipulate the perceptions of others. Finally, we will look to what is possible once you understand how they work, and examine how to best cope with them, control them, battle with them, and manipulate them.

It is hoped that by the end of the book, you will have a much better understanding of this personality, and how to deal with it in your own life. But before we can arrive there, you will have to process the idea that others can think vastly different from how you do, that things which elicit one emotion in you can elicit a vastly different emotion in others, and that in such individuals, remarkably subtle emotional stimuli, introduced in certain ways, can yield amazingly out-sized effects.

Chapter One

Rejoice _____

The chances are, if you are reading this, you have plumbed the depths of misery, through your interactions with a narcissist. In the beginning, you thought they were normal, and maybe even fun. As time went on, like the proverbial frog in a slowly heated pot of water, you failed to notice as things got bad. Suddenly one day, your life was a nightmare. You were enduring misery on a regular basis, you viewed misery as a normal part of life, and you had even forgotten what real joy was.

Before we begin, I want you to understand, you are lucky. If you are reading this, then you know the narcissist is bad, and that they are not normal. In making that realization you have taken the first step to freedom. Many who walk your path never find their way to that clarity, or the redemption you enjoy. Some suddenly find themselves succumbing to murder at the hands of their defectives, only realizing at the last moment the lies they had believed, and the moments and pleasures lost. Others never find out, living lives of endless misery and horror, and then dying, without ever knowing true beauty, true joy, true love, or true happiness. Their lives are tragic beyond words.

You however, are here. Before you is a world with sunny beaches, the smell of fresh cut grass on a spring morning breeze, and pockets of happy people - people who derive happiness from helping others and seeing them pleased. Even if you are still trapped in a relationship with the narcissist at this moment, you have all that before you. It is all just a matter of charting your course from where you are to it.

Best of all, your eyes are now open, and you can never be trapped helplessly in the pit of hell you once blindly slogged through, and viewed as a normal part of life. Honestly, I have no idea how those who do not know what the narcissist is, ever set out into the world. They are as naked and vulnerable as a newborn infant. By contrast, you are a heavily armed warrior, with all of Eden before you. Rejoice.

The most important thing to recognize right now however, is that no matter how bad things are now, you can find your way to paradise. It is out there waiting for you, and there is a path from where you are to it. The way life is structured, you get as many tries as you need to pursue paradise, and failures don't mean that you will be permanently barred from entry. Those failures only mean that you need to try once more. Never doubt the rewards of persistence and commitment, and never give up. There is nothing as sweet as a narcissist-free life of paradise, and you have taken the first, and biggest, step towards it.

Chapter Two

Where You Are, and Where You Will Go

Since you are reading this book, we will assume you are presently dealing with a narcissist. Assuming your narcissist is bad, (which they probably are, if you even briefly spotted the monster behind their mask and sought out this work), and assuming that you have just begun to figure them out, you are now in the tunnel. While you are in the tunnel, you will see the light ahead. You will know something different is approaching, you will assume it has to be better than what you have now, but you most likely do not know exactly what it is at this point, or even if you will make it to it. It is a confusing place.

To begin with, most of your memories now, in reality, only have faint shreds of evidence supporting them. Their entire foundation, the assumptions that they are built upon, are probably totally faulty. Your narcissist was never loyal. They never loved you unconditionally, and that misconception that they would never hurt you or screw you over? It was totally wrong. As a result, any memory that has preserved the Narcissist's actions, in the context of them being human and caring, is a faulty memory.

You know most of "what" happened, but the equally important "why" behind it all, will have been written into your memory by your brain, based on numerous false assumptions. This will suddenly make all of your memories seemingly suspect and faulty. If, at the time these memories were written, you assumed that your narcissist was human, the parts of your memory that were filled in by your brain, based upon that assumption, will have been total fabrications.

As a result, after your escape, you are in the strange predicament of confronting the fact that due to their faulty foundations, all of your memories may very well be fabrications. Your narcissist didn't accidentally break that treasured family heirloom, and feel bad about it afterward. She actually broke it on purpose, feigned remorse, and then laughed to herself later, behind your back, about how gullible and stupid you were for forgiving her reflexively, and not understanding how she had lashed out at you and reveled in your unhappiness. Or your narcissist didn't really buy you those flowers on your first date to make you happy – they did it to crassly manipulate you into a relationship, so they could get control over you, and then abuse you for their pleasure – and they laughed at how stupid you were for falling for it. Your narcissist didn't accidentally screw up that business deal while trying to help you. They sabotaged it specifically to screw you – and then laughed at you behind your back afterward.

When forming memories, context is vital, and since you lacked that critical piece of information (namely that your narcissist was a completely inhuman nutjob), you will now need to go back, and review all of your memories, so your brain can correct that context, and then re-store those memories in the back of your mind correctly. Until you do that, it is like waking up from a coma and finding out that you led a stunning life, but having no memory of it. It is even as if someone erased the past that you remember living, and now they are telling you that you led a life that you don't remember. Even worse, the someone telling you this is your own brain, and the argument they are making is the logic that you yourself are following to that conclusion. They are right.

In my experience, if you dealt with your narcissist for a substantial period of time, it can take up to a year or two for your brain to review the vast majority of your memories, rewrite them with the appropriate context, and then restore them in your brain. In the interim, it is as if you lived a dream, woke up, and are now being told that the past that you lived through never happened and everything you remember was a fantasy. Even worse, the real life that you lived is one you couldn't possibly believe. Each memory, suddenly re-remembered, in its appropriate context, is its own little surprise. It is a dizzying ride.

Fortunately, you probably have clear memories of all the situations that need to be rewritten. Often in these situations, little things seemed off, and as a result your brain stored the memory clearer than most. You were sure you recorded that TV show you didn't want to miss, and yet the tape inexplicably had some weird PBS crap accidentally recorded over your show. Or some item you treasured suddenly disappeared one day, and was never seen again. Or your narcissist borrowed your new car, and then had an accident which you couldn't believe they would have. Often there will be things you disregarded, scattered throughout your memory, but which you never paid much mind to, because if your narcissist was on your side, there had to be some innocent and boring explanation. All of those memories are going to have to be called up, rewritten, and re-stored.

As this is occurring, you may feel bad for ejecting the narcissist from your life. People write me while in this transition period, feeling guilty for breaking their ties to the narcissist. Inside, they still have a reflexive emotional desire to be loyal to the narcissist. They still have an emotional drive to couch his attacks on them as a product of a sickness he can't control – one for which he should be pitied and forgiven. This is natural, since your memory bank is still filled with many flawed memories of a loyal narcissist who would have stood by you, and who you should stand by, yourself. But those memories are defective. The reality is that your narcissist is a monster so bad, that despite every faulty memory you have, telling you to be loyal to him, you can't be around him for one more second. That is an awfulness which deserves no sympathy.

As the memory re-writing process comes to a close, you will near the exit of the tunnel, and begin to see the narcissist clearly. They will appear as a robot, sent from somewhere, with the sole purpose of screwing you over, and you will be amazed that you thought you owed them any loyalty, ever. Why they are like that will initially still remain a mystery, but it will gradually diminish with time and a greater understanding of them.

At that point, you will remember everything as it really happened, and your brain may finally begin to relax, feeling that it has, at last, gotten a firm grasp on this bizarre series of events, and patched up the security holes in your defenses which allowed this tragedy to occur in the first place. It is a long process, and even decades later you may suddenly have a long-lost memory pop-up, feel shock at how bizarre the truth behind it was, and then have to re-store it in the proper context. On the bright side, in the end, after this process, you should end up fairly well armored against further attack in the future.

5

One other effect often seen on nearing the end of the tunnel, is a reactivation of your perception of time, and a consequent re-expansion of one's perception of time. There is a structure in the brain called the amygdala, which registers the presence of important elements in your environment, including negativity and adversity. We will discuss it in more detail, later. This structure can, with constant negative stimulation, begin to shut off to protect your brain from the negativity.

Narcissists are noxious. Noxiousness is their weapon and they use it freely, whether they are yelling during a rage episode, dwelling on misery, or just radiating the noxious aura that surrounds them. When exposed to that much noxiousness, over time, the brain structure which registers important stimuli can become overwhelmed, and begin to shut off. The objective of shutting off is to protect you from the noxiousness around you, since if it is shut off, it can't register just how noxious your environment is. To steal an example from Scott Peck's *People of the Lie*, if you see one mangled dead body it will be shocking. If you end up on a massive battlefield for months, you may see hundreds per day for weeks, and you will gradually become numb to the shock, until you no longer notice any of that negative stimulus. Most people will perform the same protective defense, to shield themselves from the narcissist.

The effect of this is that the structure which registers important elements of your environment, and focuses you upon them, actually goes offline, leaving you deadened to the world. I had an acquaintance who actually said openly that he could not think around the narcissist I knew, named Bob. Whenever this acquaintance was around Bob, his brain felt as if it went offline, and he would begin to zone out. Even at family gatherings, when he wanted to pay attention to a conversation and take part in it, he couldn't focus his mind on what what being said, if Bob was in the area, because his brain would actually turn itself off, to protect him. The second he left Bob's presence he could feel his brain come back online, and he could concentrate easily again. I have experienced similar effects around Bob, though not having known him from my earliest childhood, I suspect the effects are greatly muted compared to my acquaintance's.

The effect of a brain that has gone offline is to leave the individual that is afflicted in a sort of waking coma. Not registering events around themselves is akin to not experiencing them due to lack of consciousness. The primary result is a memory bank which has not been

6

filled with the quantity of data which a normal passage of time should normally have filled it with. The result of this is an individual who experiences the passage of time as being unusually compressed. Events which occur years prior, only seem to have accrued a month's worth of memories in the intervening period. Ask such an individual when it feels like the attacks of September 11th happened, and they may say a year ago instead of almost a decade and a half ago. Hurricane Katrina will seem to have occurred around the same time, though it was actually five years after September 11th.

A secondary effect is a dulling of the world. When the brain structure which notices stimuli, assigns import, and focuses you upon it goes offline to avoid noticing noxious stimuli, it takes all sorts of other stimuli with it. Blue skies, fluffy white clouds, gentle breezes carrying the smell of fresh-cut grass, buzzing honeybees, warm sunshine, and beautiful people, will all tend to pass by without being noticed. In *People of the Lie,*[1] Scott Peck describes kids being raised by narcissists as having dead eyes, and always looking at the floor. What a professional would view as simply a sign of depression, was actually those kids attempting to shield their amygdala from an environment that their brain had simply come to assume would always be filled with noxious stimuli. In the process, they were missing all of the beauty of the world, failing to store memories which would reflect this, and failing to draw normal enjoyment from a world which is fundamentally wonderful and beautiful.

The good news is, if you are reading this you are, at worst, in the tunnel. That means the light is approaching, and your narcissist will hopefully be out of your environment before long. On removing your narcissist from your environment, your brain should come online of its own, and if it does not it should take minimal effort to bring it back online.

The difference between the narcissist environment and the narcissist-free environment is staggering. As your brain comes back online, and begins looking at the world around you again, you will be awed by its beauty. You will notice the things that you missed, from pretty flowers, to beautiful landscaping, to the smiles of friendly strangers. Smells will seem more intense, colors will seem brighter, and

---

[1]   Peck, S. (1985). *People of the Lie.* New York City, NY: Touchstone.

sensations, like that of sunshine on your skin will become more intense and pleasurable, as your brain again begins to open itself to experiencing the world.

As you begin to notice more, you will begin to store more memories, and this will cause the passage of time to seemingly decompress. Where the years flew by before, you will begin to see a year pass, and be astonished at how much occurred during it. You will hear of something which happened a year back, and marvel that it didn't happen five or six years back. You have everything to look forward to, in this beautiful world that you are blessed to live in.

However for now, you are probably still in the tunnel, perhaps even locked in war with your narcissist. So for now, you need intelligence on your enemy. Who they are, how they think, what to expect from them, and most importantly, where their weaknesses lie.

Chapter Three

_Projection, Reality, and Confusion_____

The biggest problem you will confront when trying to understand the narcissist is that you are decent and logical. To get inside their head, you must purge your urges towards decency, and grasp that the narcissist untethered themselves from logic and reality long ago. You have to invert every urge you feel. Imagine reason and logic as being impossible for your brain to process, and envision yourself disregarding it totally, for that reason.

This inability to understand the minds of others can be a problem for the narcissist too, however. Untethered from logic and reality, and slave to a panic that they can only tame through pure adherence to fantasy and total illogicality, the narcissist can be as ignorant of the motives driving those normal people around them as you are of their psychology.

My favorite narcissist, Bob, routinely told those around them that they were clueless. Those around him laughed, because Bob often seemed the very definition of clueless himself. He damaged and broke things, ranging from wine glasses, to statues, to vases, to furniture, everywhere he went. He routinely destroyed anything positive that would produce happiness in his family members and friends, from crashing a new car borrowed from a family member, to ruining a business deal that would have enriched him, as well as his relatives.

Yet, all of these strange things Bob did, were done purposefully, because there was no pain so vicious to Bob as the sight of family member's around him happy and contented.

I always assumed the mother of evil was selfishness. True evil would hurt others, and even not care about the hurt, because all it could think of was its own ends. But if evil had to confront a choice, between hurting others and hurting itself, or pursuing its own interests and seeing others benefit, evil would choose to help others, and in so doing, further its own ends. I thought selfishness and a desire to succeed personally would always win out. That belief was wholly naive.

There is research which shows that the psychology you confront is actually pained by the sight of happiness in others. It experiences joy in the face of others who are hurt. Imagine yourself, seeing a loved relative thrive wildly. You would feel joy. Imagine yourself, seeing a wounded puppy suffer. You would feel sorrow and anguish. In the worst narcissist, these responses are inverted. I know it seems strange, but that is only because you don't know how much they hide who they are. Few do.

These emotional responses are so strong in many narcissists, that the narcissist will sacrifice their own interests, simply to destroy happiness and bring pain and suffering to others. I would not have believed that a truly evil person existed who would sacrifice themselves, and everything they needed to survive, just to see some other people suffer. I now am shocked that I was ever so naive. That psychology is out there, and if you are reading this book, you have likely either run into it, or are dealing with it presently. It is more common than most people could imagine.

When Bob did things which, if purposeful, would have destroyed his relationships, I never thought it possible that they were purposeful. Bob needed the support of his friends and family – he needed their continued allegiance. But Bob needed something more. He needed his friends and family unhappy and miserable. So when a relative got a new car, he asked to borrow it, and crashed it. When the closing of a big business deal that would have enriched everyone was imminent, he found a way to scuttle it. When a relative had a sculpture they adored, he accidentally broke it. He did these things again and again, to the point that friends would put nice things away when he visited, and adjust their information outflow to stop him from screwing up any life changes they were planning. It was even a joke among those who knew him – he was the man who could ruin a train wreck. I even joked several times that he must carry some sort of ancient curse. Yet not once did a relative or friend stop to think that any of that might have been purposeful. In reality, it all was.

I realized later, that on several occasions, Bob would rage when things did not go perfectly for him. This is something most who deal with narcissists will see. Some small roadblock crops up in their life, and the narcissist explodes in a narcissistic rage, directed at everyone, as if the roadblock was their fault. I have since realized that in many such cases, the explosion is precipitated by the narcissist's projection of their own psychology on those around them. This leads the narcissist to believe that the small roadblock in their life was intentionally placed by someone who would derive pleasure from their suffering, just as they derive pleasure from the suffering of others. In their mind, someone else has won, and they have lost, because all of life is solely a competition to screw your friends.

Indeed, I later realized that Bob believed everyone around him thought as he did, with perhaps a few small exceptions, who he apparently believed were highly-rare benevolent souls. Bob viewed them as idiots who were too stupid to avail themselves of the pleasure received from screwing over others - and plenty stupid enough to be used freely as abuse sponges, without fear of retribution or retaliation.

This state of affairs will give a lot of narcissists undue leeway in tormenting their social contacts, without being exposed or recognized. In my case, I failed to recognize my narcissist, because if I had been as big a screw-up as he was, and somebody such as myself extended a hand and tried to help me, I would feel forever indebted.

Even had Bob been malicious, surely he wouldn't have tried to sabotage my life, because he needed me for his own purposes. I was wholly wrong. Bob needed to see those around him miserable. Everything else in his life was meaningless by comparison.

Before you can truly close the door on this phase of your life, you need to come to terms with the fact that these people are truly, purely evil. Inside, I suspect many who read this are saying, "*Well, my narcissist isn't that bad – what is being described here is a rare case.*" Be aware that I have been at that stage too, and it is the first step. For a normal person, merely accepting the existence of such a psychology is a huge step indeed, and you have not made it by accident. Keep your eyes open, ruminate on everything you see, and continue down the rabbit hole as far as logic and reason will take you. If your narcissist was bad enough to have you seek out this book, you will be amazed at how far down you will end up.

Chapter Four

A Word of Caution _____

Narcissists are designed and trained through extensive experience, from their earliest childhoods, to hide who they are, and keep you from spotting them. But if you are here, you cracked their code, and spotted yours. That is actually unusual - and a cause for concern.

I believe the vast majority of narcissists don't get spotted. They get married, raise families, even screw up their kids and destroy the happiness of their spouses - but they don't get caught. Your's got caught. Why? It may be that their problem is so severe, that it couldn't be hidden.

Narcissists are the Mozarts of deception. From their earliest ages, when they revealed the evil within, they were punished – by their teachers, by their peers, and by their family. As a result, they were trained to a prodigy level, from their earliest ages, to hide who they are. For that reason, I liken a person who spotted their narcissist to a music-composing neophyte who just out-composed a Mozart-level prodigy by accident. Either you were incredibly lucky, or your Mozart was composing his deception under the impossibly severe handicap of a personality so defective and noxious that even a prodigy couldn't hide it.

Severe narcissists can be killers, especially as their deceptions become unraveled, and they begin to feel a threat of exposure. They can, and many do, kill wives who intend to leave them, family members who they see as threats to their reputations within the family, even employers who threaten to fire them and place a stain of failure on their work history.

One person who came to me for advice, said of their narcissist, *"He would never be properly violent within the family."* This was something which scared me, because it was emblematic of the normal psychology facing the narcissist, and the handicap that the normal person operates under. A normal person thinks that the narcissist has been open with them about who they are, all along. A normal person thinks that killing someone who is seen as a threat, is an honest affair. You tell them you are angry, get a tire iron, go to their house, wait on their front porch, and then walk up to them and hit them when they come home. Even worse, they assume that they can make an assessment based upon what the narcissist has shown them to date. Narcissists don't operate that way.

A narcissist smiles, tells you how happy they are with you, and gives you a screwdriver mixed with methyl alcohol instead of vodka. Then he acts tormented with grief as you succumb in the hospital. A narcissist spends an hour under your car fatiguing your worn brake lines, so when they break, it isn't clear they've been cut. Then they act extra nice, helping you load your car before your big trip.

Narcissist don't get properly violent. If they intend to get violent, they try to kill you in a way that if they fail, you never even knew they tried, and nobody is the wiser - and if they succeed, nobody knows that what happened was due to them. They do it, out of the blue, with no warning, when you least think it likely, in a cowardly way you wouldn't expect. Off the top of my head, I can think of one guy who gave the methyl-alcohol laced screwdriver to his wife, another who gave her husband a milkshake sweetened with antifreeze, another who drove real fast, reached over, unbuckled his wife's seat belt, and then crashed his car into a tree, killing her, another guy who beat his wife to death, loaded her in the car, and then crashed it to make it look like an accident, another guy who filled his own house with carbon monoxide, by screwing with the heating system, killing his wife, while he read a book in a room with an open window, and another guy who killed his wife by messing with her scuba air supply on a dive, without her knowing. None of those victims suspected that their narcissist would get properly violent, and I am sure all would have been shocked to learn the truth, before they were killed. That is how it works with the Mozarts of deception.

If you have spotted your narcissist, you have no idea who they are - only that evil is within them. You have scratched their surface, and seen something evil in the scratch. How deep that evil runs is a mystery,

14

because the evil you saw was a small part of all the evil that your narcissist is hiding. If you've spotted your narcissist, it probably runs quite deep, and may even run right to the core. They could be plotting your demise right now, and you wouldn't know it, because you can't know exactly how damaged they are, until they try to kill you.

Of course there is a wide spectrum of behavior between doing nothing and murder, and anything on that spectrum is a possibility, on your narcissist's list of options. They might merely contaminate your food with a low dose of a heavy metal toxin, to make you just sick enough that you can't work, so you will be dependent upon them for care and money. Or they might try to give you the flu, by rubbing an infected colleague's Kleenex on your dinner plate when they get home from work. They might sabotage a work project you brought home, in the hopes of getting you fired, so you will need them for support, more than ever.

They may even damage themselves in the process of attacking you, to establish the ridiculousness of accusing them of attacking you purposefully. The woman above, who gave her husband antifreeze, lost the means of support for her family when he died. The guy who crashed his own car after unbuckling his wife's seat belt sustained serious injuries himself. The guy who filled his own house with Carbon Monoxide argued, correctly, that it could have killed him, so he would never have done it. To a narcissist, infecting themselves with the flu, and bringing it home to infect you, is the brilliance of the plan, because to the narcissist, it renders the plan unable to be blamed upon them by any logical mind. It is the masking of the crime which will both, be paramount in the narcissist's mind, and make it almost impossible for you to see the attack coming.

If you have spotted your narcissist you must understand that being revealed will panic them, in a way you cannot imagine. Losing your dependency and the cover you offer for their defectiveness will panic them. The thought of everyone in your family realizing how defective they are, and maybe blaming them for all the things they have done, will panic them. The thought of you, off enjoying the world, and succeeding wildly, while they are left behind, worthless and alone, will panic them. All of the unpredictable changes which will threaten, should their secret be revealed, will panic them. Once they feel that panic, they might try to kill you to restore the sanctity of their secret, and thereby shut off that panic. Exercise extreme caution.

Chapter Five

_____

Where it Begins _____

Although this section will detail a primary developmental aspect of this psychology's origins, it should not be inferred that there is no other biochemical/environmental, genetic, or epigenetic predisposition which sets the foundation, for these events to create the final noxious product that will be described in this work. Indeed, it is even possible that there is some biochemical-exposure/environmental event which occurs during gestation, which itself implants a bad seed, that these events subsequently nourish to fruition. The research is still quite unclear.

That said, whatever the material foundations of the disorder, they are merely the foundations. In the vast majority of cases, it is these foundations which allow the process described here to have its effects, and imbue itself within the narcissist's nature. In the end, your narcissist was very likely molded by events such as these, and they will define his nature, even if the molding required some other element to weaken your narcissist, erode his psychological resiliency, and allow this process to have its effects. Whatever the foundations may be of the house of horrors you now inhabit, it is the following which will prove to be the architectural blueprints of the floor plan, and it is for that reason that we will focus upon that alone. Understand the blueprint, and you will find the nearest exit much more easily.

The psychiatrist M. Scott Peck referred to narcissists as *"People of the Lie,"* a phrase which he used as the title of a book he wrote on the subject of evil. In the book *Glimpses of the Devil*,[1] he outlined a case of what he believed was actually a case of evil due to demonic possession, which he believed began when as a child, the victim chose to believe a lie, to make herself feel better. The young girl's father had sexually

_____

[1]   Peck, S. (2005). *Glimpses of the Devil.* New York City, NY: Simon and Schuster.

molested her, but rather than accept that and deal with it, she convinced herself that her father was a medical doctor who examined her, and believing this lie made her feel better about what had happened. In Peck's mind, once she was willing to believe this lie simply to make herself feel better, she was willing to believe all sorts of lies to feel better, including those of the demons that he believed then seized the opportunity of her weakened mind, and possessed her.

Although the nuances of demonology are beyond the scope of this book, my own narcissist, Bob, seemed to have a similar genesis, one that I believe is probably relatively common to the psychology.

In Bob's case, at age seven, he was forced to wear a back-brace to school, due to a spine which curved forward very profoundly. His physician believed this was a structural issue with the vertebrae and muscles which required the corrective effects of a physical restraint, however in Bob's case, I suspect the curvature was likely more psychological in origin.

As an adult, when angered or threatened, Bob would reflexively flex his gluteal muscles in his posterior, thrusting his hips forward. Simultaneously he would flex his abdominal muscles, pulling the front of his rib cage downward, towards the front of his hips. This, combined with pulling his head forward and down defensively, would bend his spine into what, from the side, appeared to be a gross "C"-shaped deformity of his spine. It would be accompanied by his arms hanging outward at an angle to the sides of his body, overly straightened, with clenched fists, and a facial expression of extreme hatred. It seemed to be a position that he assumed subconsciously in response to being angered. I assume that he probably felt threatened in the doctor's office as a child, assumed that position, and the doctor's immediate response on seeing him was to prescribe the back-brace.

The back-brace the physician prescribed was highly restrictive. It basically had the same effect as fusing together the bones of his hips, all of his vertebrae up through his neck to his skull, and his shoulder bones. It not only prevented any forward curvature of the spine, but it also prevented any twisting motions, such as one would use to turn around, from his hips, up through his neck and skull.

Whereas once, he could have turned around at the waist to look behind him, now he was bound into a structure which forbade all twisting and turning. Even his head was strapped tightly into the brace, which extended up around his skull, preventing him from turning his neck to see behind him. Walking suddenly went from a fluid, easy motion, to an awkward balancing of a stiff upper body which had no ability to perform the small adjustments we all take for granted when balancing and moving. Whereas seeing what was behind him previously required a quick turn of the head, it now required an awkward, bouncing dance, as his feet shuffled and rotated his whole body, until his feet were pointed 180 degrees around, to directly face what he was interested in.

The children at the school didn't like Bob, but I am not sure why. Perhaps the postural issue was a symptom of a deeper issue with anger, perhaps he had been mean from the beginning, I don't know. He was reportedly unkind to his family, even as a child, so he was probably a bad seed from the start. Regardless of the motives, once Bob was thrust onto the playground, bound in a back-brace, and unable to defend himself, the children began to swarm him. Those behind him would kick him in the calves, while those in front taunted him. As he turned to confront those kicking him, they fled, and disappeared into the mass of children. Those remaining, who he now faced, taunted him, as those who he had turned from began running up and kicking his calves.

The teachers never intervened, possibly because he had a propensity for bullying other children, and so this torment went on for the entire recess. Bob was endlessly tormented, his tormenters always managed to escape into the crowd, and none ever suffered any consequence for their actions.

As an adult, Bob would throw raging narcissistic tantrums. His back bent onto a C-shape, he would stomp around, his feet moving strangely, as if his body were restrained by an imaginary back-brace. His hands were held in front of him, and shaken up and down together, as he made an inhuman, growling roar, his face frozen in an almost inhuman expression of rage. It was quite a sight. Thinking back to these scenes, I could see a child doing that, as the crowd around him went wild with euphoric mirth and laughter. I suspect it is how the torments of his childhood climaxed, to the glee of the surrounding crowd, who likely only redoubled their efforts the next day, to produce that epic spectacle.

After the torments of his recess ended, Bob would return to the classroom, where he would apparently stew over what had happened.

Around him, the other children were probably euphoric, poking each other and laughing at the wild scene they had just precipitated. Bound by his brace, trapped in his desk, Bob could do nothing, and worse, he knew it would happen all over again tomorrow, and again the day after. He had no ability to escape his predicament.

So strained, his brain would play, over and over again, the torments past, and imagine the torments to come. Again and again, it would feel the rage and painful psychological agony of the past, mixed with the terror of contemplating the future. Quickly, his brain's ability to maintain its operations would begin to actually break down. From his description, it began with what would best be classified as an *optical migraine.* Within his visual field, a small prismatic disturbance would begin in the outer margins of the upper right quadrant of his field of vision. As the minutes passed, the prismatic disturbance would spread downward in a crescent shape, and then gradually spread into the central area of his field of vision, and outward to the other side. It would essentially turn his visual field into a distorted blur of prismatic lights and colors, and this would basically blind him for a short period. As it began, he would quickly head to the nurse's office, and within a short time, he would be violently ill, suffering agonizing headaches and throwing up uncontrollably, over and over.

His mother would come and take him home from school. He begged her to not make him wear the back brace, but she said it was medically necessary, and that was that. There at home, he would contemplate the torments he endured, and the torments he would face the next day on his return. He thought of everyone, from the children who tortured him, to the teachers who didn't stop it, to his mother who made it all happen, and he seethed with hatred for all of them.

If he continued to contemplate the torments, and faced the reality that he could not alter, he would again grow sick, and experience all of the agonizing physical symptoms precipitated by his gross anxiety. It was here that I believe Bob learned to deny reality, as a means of controlling his own mind's perceptions, and emotions. It was here, that Bob became one of Scott Peck's *People of the Lie.*

When you are young, your brain exhibits what neurobiologists call plasticity – that means your brain is unusually adaptable, and able to mold itself to do whatever it is called upon to do. It is why a child exposed to music will often grow up to be unusually talented at it and why we all learn languages effortlessly when we are young. It is even why a child with an eye disorder blocking light from their retina will end up essentially blind for life, unless the eye is fixed when they are very young. If you fix it when they are older, the eye is larger and easier to operate on. However, once fixed, although light will then hit their retina, their brain will be unable to process the signals this produces into vision. The loss of brain plasticity with age will actually prevent the growth and development of the brain structures necessary to do the processing. Either it is fixed early so the brain can develop the brain structure to process the signals into vision while they are young, or the older brain will lose the ability to develop the structure necessary to turn light signals into vision, and fixing the eye will offer very little benefit.

As Bob repeated this tragedy each day, day after day, it was as if he were exercising a stress/panic/agony muscle in his brain, at the very time when such exercise would maximize the growth and development of this structure. Each day, he was doing fifty sets of fifty reps of stressing - and his brain's stress muscle grew. Where normal kids triggered their stress and felt stress, Bob's stress muscle could throttle his entire brain at the most minor of stresses. His plastic brain had adapted into a stress engine, the likes of which few people could imagine. Foist any negativity upon him and his brain would so panic, that it would stop processing visual signals, his stomach would lose the ability to function, he would vomit, and his head would actually throb with stress. If he could deny the reality of his world, and convince himself of a fantasy where nothing could be done to him however, his symptoms would all abate.

This leads to one of the more puzzling facets of the narcissist - his ability to believe anything, at any moment, if it suits his purposes. Bob once did something in front of me which was very illogical. When I asked him about it the next day, his response was *"Not only didn't I do that – I would never do anything like that!"* His voice rose to a crescendo and his arms waved, to emphasize how certain he was, of the impossibility of his even contemplating what he had done right in front of me.

For a moment, I stood befuddled. It honestly appeared as if Bob actually believed that he could never do anything so illogical as what he had done. If that was true, this was huge, because the incident in

21

question was so illogical and crazy, that it was not something that any normal person could forget having done. Did Bob have some sort of Multiple Personality Disorder? Did another personality named Joe do the thing yesterday, and today Bob not only has no recollection of it, he thinks he could never do it, because he couldn't? Who have I been dealing with each day?

What I had encountered was the narcissist's false reality. Basically the narcissist doesn't have a concrete sense of what has happened in the past. Rather the narcissist defines past events fluidly and vaguely, making up memories on the fly, so as to render their own memory of the past as unstressful to their brain as possible. They don't remember to remember – they remember in such a way as to first, protect themselves from the agony. This is actually an acquired ability, carefully practiced since youth, and developed to allow the narcissist to avoid the uncomfortable agony that they experience when contemplating unpleasantness.

Since accepting that he had done something illogical would have made Bob uncomfortable, Bob simply told himself he had never done it, and that was that. Not only had he never done it, he would never do anything even remotely similar! Believing that made Bob feel better about himself and his grip on logic and reality, so he told himself it was true, and whatever memories he had of the event were either ignored or suppressed.

This ability almost certainly first arose, as Bob lay there as a child, in bed, pondering the fate he would face the next day at school. If he accepted reality and acknowledged it, his brain would violently punish him with all the physical symptoms that he now experienced when stressed. But if he could have denied that reality, and simply believed whatever made him feel good, he could have shut off the symptoms, and enjoyed at least a temporary respite from the agony. To work, however, he had to learn to actually believe the lies that he told himself. Once he began to acquire this trait, given how his brain stressed epically at the most minor events, it was a slippery slope. Pretty soon, he would be denying all sorts of negative realities. As he denied more realities, his brain became less accustomed to acclimating to stress, and ever more realities would need to be denied. Soon he would be fleeing from a stalking panic which would drive him ever deeper into his world of fantasy.

Eventually, as his ability to cope with stress atrophied and eroded, that fantasy would out of necessity, grow proactive, and he would begin to actively visualize himself as his *"false-self"* – perfect in every regard. This would occur, because by that point, any hint of negativity would set off his panic response – a response he had lost all ability to cope with. He did not see himself as perfect because it made him feel good. He saw himself as perfect because to do anything else would result in a pain that he couldn't tolerate. This was a last ditch attempt to salvage some semblance of emotional normalcy from the neurological wreckage that was his brain. It was done out of panicked necessity.

Until you grasp this facet of narcissist psychology, and understand how it arises, their adherence to a false reality can be a very confusing part of dealing with a narcissist. Once you grasp where it comes from however, you have pulled at that first thread that holds together the complex tapestry that is their cognitive model. As you continue to pull on that thread, the tapestry will unravel, and you will begin to see how every facet of their mind works.

Now one should not ignore one other trait which arose from Bob's early conditioning experiences. Wherever Bob looked, he saw people that he hated. He was the man who felt nothing but hate. There were the kids who tormented him. There were the teachers who allowed it. There was his mother who made him wear the brace, and his father who didn't intervene. There was the doctor, and the therapist who showed his mom how to use the brace. Even the strangers on the street were contemptible, because they went happily about their lives, ignoring him, while he was forced to suffer alone. I suspect Bob never looked at anyone with appreciation or love at that age, so he never grew to feel bound to anyone in that way. Everyone was an enemy.

As we wrote, when you are young, your brain develops the abilities it will need as an adult, based upon what you call upon it to do as a child. If called upon to do something, the brain will develop the ability to do it unusually well. In Bob's case, it developed the ability to produce a perpetual, extraordinarily strong hatred and anger for everyone around him. I view it as having the *"angry switch"* in your head, which is normally turned on in response to normally angering stimuli, broken off in the *"on"* position. From that moment forward, all you will feel is anger at everyone and everything, regardless of the logical reasons mitigating against it – and your brain will develop the ability to feel that anger unusually strongly.

I came across this attitude in another narcissist online once. In an article pondering if narcissist's know they are narcissists, a narcissist commented that, *"I am a vengeful narcissist and I stick my middle finger to the world and say F#CK YOU ALL. I celebrate myself because I survived YOU..."*[1] In that moment of accidental honesty, that narcissist summed up what is really going on in your narcissist's head – and why they can be so dangerous.

That statement is that narcissist's brain, frozen in the childhood environment which formed it, by neural pathways burned into it all those years ago. That is a mindset common to the disorder, because it is produced by the childhood conditions that generate it. Have no doubt, that narcissist hides that worldview from everyone he is close to, even as he views them as the tormenters who forever destroyed his love for the world, and seeks his vengeance on them. If you have a narcissist, this is what he is hiding from you. It is inherent to the disorder.

Interestingly, narcissist's seem to assume that their hatred is an accurate characterization of the state of the world, and that anyone who doesn't exhibit it against others, is somehow ignorant of a fundamental, underlying truth about the world. Since everyone is an enemy, they learn to hide this attitude from those around them, as a way of fitting in and functioning in the world, and they appear to assume that similarly, most everyone else, with the exception of a few isolated rubes, is faking their empathy with the world as well. I doubt a full Narcissist can imagine love, loyalty, or the pleasure that normal people get from seeing friends happy.

In short, Bob's entire syndrome, from his hatred and envy for everyone, to his development of a false reality, to his deceptive actions, appeared to have arisen from the traumatic events of his past, and his inability to process them without experiencing an extraordinary level of pain and suffering. The thoughts and emotions produced by that incident developed his hatred and loathing as if it were a muscle, even as it

---

[1] Reader Comments on Kaufman, S. B. (2011). "Do Narcissists Know They Are Narcissists?" <http://www.psychologytoday.com/blog/beautiful-minds/201103/do-narcissists-know-they-are-narcissists/comments> (Accessed 20 May, 2014).

24

developed his ability to make up, on the fly, a perception of past reality which would minimize the negative stresses he experienced.

As we progress through this work, you will be continually exposed to this idea that the narcissist's entire malady is an adaptive mechanism designed to minimize this internal panic sensation that they feel. It is important to understand this idea, because if the narcissist is exhibiting their aberrant behavior in an effort to avoid a horrific terror that they cannot face, it should alert you to the fact that they are capable of anything, and normalcy is not an option. They are not weakly driven to hurt by a weak pleasure that they weakly want to feel when doing it. They are uncontrollably driven to hurt by a horrific terror which they cannot possibly face, and which they can only escape by inflicting pain. They are uncontrollably evil, and capable of anything.

Do not allow your narcissist's false imitations of normalcy to fool you into thinking that their evil is merely a choice, or blind you to the idea that they are capable of anything - even the inhuman.

Chapter Six

The Amygdala and the
Belief of Lies _____

Within the brain is a specific brain structure called the amygdala. An understanding of the amygdala is crucial to an understanding of the narcissist, for it is likely that it is the amygdala which narcissists have, in essence, "hacked," altering its neurological function to suit their own purposes.

The function the amygdala performs, is best described as being like the function of Captain Kirk on the Starship Enterprise, from the old TV show Star Trek. Captain Kirk sits in the big chair on the bridge, with all the TV screens and data before him. He focuses on what is important among all of that data, and then directs someone to deal with it for him. He may not know engineering, but the part of his ship which handles engineering is a few feet away and it still reports all of its data to him, as well as its analysis and recommendations. Just like your amygdala, Captain Kirk decides what is important among all of the data he is presented, and what should be done about it. He may not be a communications specialist, but he has someone for that who is right at hand, just as he does for every other specialty, from medicine, to security, to Spock's inimitable logic.

Likewise, the amygdala does not perform logic functions, or visual processing, or auditory sensing and processing, but all of these areas of the brain loosely report to the amygdala, and it scans through all the data, often even before you are consciously aware of it. It scans everything which you notice, from external stimuli to internal ideas, and even some data you don't consciously notice, and it decides what you will focus on.

It even calls up the sensations that what you focus upon will elicit. Due to the fact that it calls up fear and anxiety when fear and anxiety are appropriate to a given stimulus, it is often thought of as producing fear and anxiety, but the truth is it is much more of a central processing center that focuses your sentience, than strictly an anxiety center. (Indeed, there is evidence that the anxiety the amygdala calls up is actually produced by another portion of a part of the brain called the Anterior Cingulate Cortex (ACC) which research notes is active during "*neural alarms.*")

So the amygdala is basically the Captain of the brain, quietly watching everything which flies across the brain's radar. When anxiety is appropriate it is the amygdala's recognition of the anxiety producing stimulus as important, and its subsequent activation of the neural alarm, which brings that anxiety to bear on the rest of the organism. It is not until the anxiety-producing stimulus is removed from the environment (and the brain's perceptual map of the environment) that the amygdala will cease producing panic – at least in normal people.

In Bob, it would appear that after being placed under a continuous, and highly bothersome stimulus, he was able, through trial and error, to discover a cognitive work-around – a sort of neurological short circuit which allowed him to replace any negative perception of reality with a more benign perception of reality that did not elicit any anxious sensations. He, in essence, hacked into his amygdala, and programmed it to ignore or deny any stimulus which was likely to elicit panic or anxiety. From that point forward, if any negative stimulus began to appear on one of his amygdala's big TV screens, his amygdala would immediately turn that screen off, and tell itself that such information was obviously incorrect, and thus to be ignored. Unfortunately, in developing this work-around, Bob also untethered his amygdala, and himself, from the reality of the world around him.

Once that cognitive workaround was present, it was destined to become the go to neural pathway for any stressful stimulus. From that moment forward, when Bob encountered a stressful stimulus, he could confront it and experience anxiety, or he could deny its existence and elicit immediate relief. Over time, Bob's brain eventually learned to avoid reality at all cost.

It trained itself, like a dog brought to heel through frequent yanks on its choke collar each time it honestly assessed reality. As his brain began avoiding reality reflexively, it honestly coped with stress ever less often. As his brain became less adapted to coping with stress, it became less able to cope with stress, minor stresses became more panicking if faced, and the yanks on his choke chain became ever more painful whenever he allowed his mind to drift in the vicinity of any reality that was negative, no matter how minor. You see where this vicious cycle leads.

For most people stress is a good thing, even though it doesn't feel that way. You encounter stress when something in your environment indicates negativity is forthcoming, and you use that stress to motivate you to avoid that negativity. For example, if you have a project to do at work, and it isn't done, then in that unfinished state, that unfinished project will end your career. That is potential negativity forthcoming. Your amygdala will flag that data for significance, and send it out to the rest of your brain for deeper analysis. The rest of your brain will extrapolate out all of the potential consequences, and feed them back to the amygdala, which will apply anxiety in response to the projected outcome of job-loss.

As you map out potential behaviors to perform, the anxiety will continue whenever you think about any option which will perpetuate that project's unfinished state. That anxiety will drive you to rummage through your brain in search of cognitive relief, and eventually your brain will find an option which will finish the job. Once you alter your amygdala's read of reality, such that the job is on its way to being finished, your amygdala will no longer see danger, and you will not experience stress. Once the job is finished, your amygdala will see no negativity forthcoming from its state, it will ignore it completely, and you will feel all the stress evaporate into thin air.

Normal people encounter stress when something in their environment is bad. They remove the stress from their life by removing the environmental variable producing it, and this makes their environment less potentially negative for them. As strange as it sounds, for most people, stress, used properly, can make their life immeasurably better.

Unfortunately, Bob's brain didn't work that way. When he encountered negativity, it had become so traumatic that he denied it was possible, and thus he never had the ability to structure his life in such a way as to become successful – at work, with friends, in his family, or even as a person. As time went on, his environment became ever more negative, and he retreated ever farther into his bubble of denial – his hyper-sensitive amygdala retreating behind ever more false reality. Even confronting his self-inflicted cognitive shortcoming became stressful, so eventually he learned to tell himself that every bad thing which happened was inflicted upon him by everyone else. Although his hatred and bitterness for everyone only grew, that anger was minimal compared to confronting the fact that his brain was fundamentally faulty, and he needed to start confronting reality or more negativity would be in his future.

It is worth noting that in some research, electrical stimulation of the amygdala (a gross simulation of neural activity) has produced anger. One woman, who was so stimulated, reported feeling so angry that she wanted to just start breaking things and hitting people, and couldn't control it. In narcissists you have individuals who seem to have unusually sensitive amygdalae, which are not well adapted to shut off their stimulation through normal behaviors designed to produce environmental modification. We discussed in the previous chapter how plasticity likely contributes to the development of an angry baseline mood in the narcissist. It is also worth noting (particularly in light of the phenomenon of narcissistic rage) that such a baseline mood is almost certainly exacerbated by any minor amygdala stimulation. Thus if you have an individual, imbued with a strong anger reflex, then applying any stress to their hyper-sensitive amygdala could easily cause a boiling over of anger, and a consequent narcissistic rage. We will discuss this more when we discuss the amygdala hijack, and how it allows you to disable narcissist brains.

Bob still wanted to be seen as normal despite all of these handicaps, however. He wanted what other people wanted, namely a wife, a house, a job, and all the other stuff. But to try to get those, he needed to don a mask which hid the hatred he had inside. He needed to act normal.

Beneath his mask, that hatred festered, and looked for any opportunity to relieve itself, sometimes almost comically. I remember Bob once letting slip his contempt for his mom during one instance when he was relieving his anger by raging at her. Bob had been part of a marching band. During an important performance, he purposely marched out of step to screw up the whole thing for everyone. His mother, ever the loving mom, commented to family on how amazing it was that

30

everyone was out of step but him. Bob recounted her statement with utter contempt for her stupidity. To Bob, who had tried to screw the entire marching band by destroying their performance, she was the idiot, for being so stupid that she had no idea what he had been doing.

Bob's tortured genesis brings to mind one other observation in passing. It is tempting on reading this analysis to be sympathetic towards him. However, I suspect within him was always a kernel of a real evil. He enjoyed the suffering of others, in a way I tend to think was innate. I suspect it was why when he was placed in the back brace, all of the other children converged on him. It is also why it affected him so deeply, that he developed a full blown personality disorder.

When I finally realized what Bob was, and cataloged all his traits, I realized that he had many psychological traits of a serial killer. Yet to my knowledge, he never took a victim. (Honestly, it would not surprise me at all, if tomorrow I found out that he had taken several.)

Although I do not condone bullying, I strongly suspect that when an entire crowd ostracizes a child to the extent Bob was ostracized, something inside that child may be likely to be evil, and it may be that kernel of evil that the crowd is focusing upon. It is even possible that this is some ancient, evolved, group behavior, designed to train those who are evil, at an early age, to constrain their evil as an adult, lest they again find themselves at the center of an angry mob.

Had Bob not developed an intense fear of the crowd turning on him, I suspect he would have developed his hatred for everyone, and especially happy women, all the same - just at a more gradual pace. As an adult, it is possible, that unconstrained by a fear of the mob, he might have done horrible things. There may be several young women who did not meet horrible ends, because Bob's evil was neurologically constrained by the actions of the crowd, on that playground so long ago.

It will be informative to watch, as we attempt to wholly eradicate bullying, whether we eliminate a vital social mechanism designed to imbue behavioral control among a few cognitively deviant individuals within the larger group of the "bullied." If we do, we will produce a greater share of evil people who, as adults, do not constrain their evil urges, and who engage in horrors upon others far more often.

What you will hopefully take from this chapter is an understanding of how the amygdala's ability to guide focus is related the narcissist's disorder, how its stimulation affects emotion, and that this can be used by a savvy individual to constrain the narcissist's behavior, if they know how.

Most importantly, narcissists are not narcissists because they want to be. They are narcissists because they have to be. They don't cling to delusions of omnipotence and perfection because they want to. They do so because to even vaguely touch upon any possibility of anything else, is to trigger the hyper-sensitive trigger on an unbearable torment that the narcissist cannot tolerate.

This is vital to understand, because it indicates that the narcissist does not operate from a position of strength. Rather, he desperately clings with oiled hands to a slippery, untenable lie, because of a terror which you can unleash upon him at will – if you know how.

Chapter Seven

The Amygdala Hijack

Many of us have seen a narcissist rage. Blind to everyone around them, they begin to explode like a volcano. Spittle flies, arms wave elaborately, sometimes they even growl like a big angry animal, all while stomping around, or doing something else that is totally crazy. If you have escaped your narcissist, and been out for a year or more, those moments can become some of your funniest memories, but if you are still trapped, they are no laughing matter.

What is the narcissistic rage? It is a behavioral manifestation of amygdala activation, triggered in response to something stressful, which activates their amygdala, and triggers an overwhelming emotional drive to act out in some way. It is not logical - the emotional drive is triggered below the conscious awareness. Deep mechanisms within the brain see something, and an uncontrollable emotional drive just wells up, forcing the narcissist to freak out. This deeply-rooted, subconsciously triggered emotional drive is the foundation of the narcissist's entire psychological condition.

The real cause can be confusing, because it can sometimes play out like this. Your narcissist is deep in thought. His thoughts drift to his grandfather, who once told him there was something wrong with him. His thoughts then turn angry, almost reflexively. *"Something wrong with me! The person who had something wrong with him was my grandfather! That no good bastard! I remember when he gave my little brother a BB gun for Christmas, and all I got was a model airplane. He did that to insult me, and make me angry. He knew I wanted a BB gun. He knew I'd see my brother using his and get jealous! He did that purposely to hurt me! And on Christmas no less! How dare he! He hurt me purposely on Christmas, and ruined my childhood!"* Once the anger switch in their brain is triggered, logic and reason give way to ever more angry thoughts and conclusions, all designed to justify the anger.

By now, your narcissist's amygdala is in quite a tizzy. Suddenly, in you walk, wearing a dress that he once said didn't suit you. His amygdala, already in high gear and full of rage, flags that dress, focuses on it, and you are off to the races. His amygdala needs relief, and so it begins to blow, by castigating you for purposely wearing a dress which makes you look stupid, and by extension makes him feel stupid in front of other people. Now he is going to justify his anger for you. That can then progress to how you are a horrible wife, how useless you are, how you hold him back, etc, etc. None of it is logical, of course, but it still has its effects.

This explosion of rage is done both, to vent his amygdala stress by making you miserable, which has a calming influence on him, and to distract him from his previous line of thought, which was only getting more bothersome to him. As long as his amygdala flags that dress as important, he focuses on it, and he vomits out his rage, he isn't thinking about his grandfather, or the irredeemable nature of his ruined childhood. He is also giving his amygdala the illusion of doing something tangible to alter his environment, so as to relieve the anger he had built up within it. Additionally, your amygdala is now getting angry, and you begin to yell and wave your hands. Your yelling and elaborate gesturing further distracts his amygdala, and provides him further relief, because he can tell himself that he is in control, and you are an angry nutjob. In short, he was in a bad place when you walked in, so he pressed buttons in your head, and used you as a giant amygdala-distracting/relieving machine, to calm himself down.

So what triggered the rage? In a word, his amygdala.

The amygdala is a fascinating organ, and the root of the vast majority of brain manipulations. When a hypnotist hypnotizes you, he is manipulating your amygdala, focusing it with visualization techniques on what he wants you to focus on. If he gets you picturing a calm, flowing stream, with soft moss by the edge, and tells you to feel relaxed as you sit by it, he is really telling your amygdala, *"Focus on this relaxing thought, relax this person, and don't let any other thoughts intrude, so I may focus them on the suggestion that I want to focus them on."*

When a pickpocket takes your wallet, he flags your amygdala with something more noticeable, but irrelevant, so your amygdala will

34

not focus on the sensation of your wallet sliding out of your pocket. He grabs your shoulder, motions toward a guy across the room, and asserts something untrue about the guy to you, as he slides your wallet out of your pocket. Your amygdala focuses first on the feel of his hand on your shoulder, follows his point to the guy across the room, and then puzzles over the incorrect statement, all of which distract you from the sensation of your wallet moving in your pocket.

A magician flags your amygdala with an ostentatious distraction and a sexy assistant, so your amygdala doesn't flag his deception and notice it. A mentalist focuses you on his one good read of your past, and diminishes the relevance of all his misreads, so you will feel as if he is psychic. The placebo effect can focus you on the thought that you will be cured, rather than your symptoms. You don't notice your ear itches after hitting your thumb with a hammer. You can't text while driving. It goes on and on.

The narcissist is all amygdala. It is always highly primed to flag negative material and draw the narcissist's entire focus to it. If it can't be immediately denied, it will then produce a massively outsized angry/fearful/panicked emotional response to it, so as to drive the relevant material from their reality, so it may then be more easily be denied. Their amygdala is on a hair trigger, and their entire psychology is an attempt to shield the amygdala from any negative stimulation.

So how did this information help me? I got through dealing with my narcissist by purposely taking his amygdala, and sending it over the edge through aggressive, purposeful stimulation. It turns out that when narcissists throw rages, they are actually trying to shut off their amygdala, to avoid what would normally come next. When they rage, that crazy, uncontrolled, behavioral explosion is a desperate attempt to prevent a state of even worse cognitive dysfunction – an agonizing brain explosion that the narcissist will do anything to avoid.

The rage is the narcissist's last-ditch desperate attempt to quiet an amygdala explosion of unimaginable proportions. Since nobody has figured this out yet, most of the time, everybody plays their proscribed role for the narcissist, and most often the rages work the way the narcissist wants them to. After throwing them, the narcissist literally feels better, as if they had vomited out all the rage in their stomach which was making them sick. In my case, by executing the amygdala

35

hijack at that moment, I sewed my narcissist's lips shut around a trash pump outlet pumping even more rage into him, and when he went to vomit, I pumped five times more rage into his belly, on top of the vomit. Basically, his brain fried right in front of me.

In my narcissist, the first time I began to do this, he became more enraged, then docile, then confused, and then quieter. After a few minutes, he complained that he was beginning to have stroke symptoms – and when I looked at him - wow, was he ever. As his brain reached epic rage levels of amygdala activity, and then surpassed that, I assume that his amygdala actually began to exhaust itself, and as a result, parts of the brain shut down, producing symptoms exactly like those of a stroke, or more accurately, a Transient Ischemic Attack. Following his subsequent medical examination, it was deemed a Transient Ischemic Attack of unknown origin, however I believe the brain was not denied sufficient levels of oxygen and nutrients due to reduced blood flow, but rather the amygdala fired off so aggressively that normal levels of nutrients and oxygen were no longer sufficient to sustain the brain's heightened operational tempo, and parts of it had to be shut down, lest they be killed off by the hypoxia.

Psychological professionals have sometimes referred to ambulatory schizophrenics - people who are fully functional normally, but who when stressed, begin to exhibit the disordered thinking patterns of a schizophrenic. Dr Peck discussed one named Sarah, in People of the Lie. He confronted her directly, about why she was so oppressive and evil to her husband. Thusly confronted, she snapped, launching into a nonsensical rant about apples and oranges, which devolved into whether Dr Peck thought that she was more reminiscent of a rough skinned orange or a smooth skinned apple, and finally calling Dr Peck an orange peeler who would end up in the garbage - *"with all the other fruits."*

The rant was the early stage of amygdala dysfunction, as her amygdala lost the ability to focus clearly on a subject, and determine what was relevant and what was not. What you got was a strange, disordered, stream-of-consciousness-diatribe, the parts of which seemed strangely unrelated, and the gist of which never seemed really clear. Dr Peck's previous line of questioning had begun to touch on an underlying trigger which set off her amygdala, and as it over-fired in panic mode, it burned up all of it's nutrients, and began to malfunction. Once malfunctioning, her amygdala could not focus on a cogent train of thought, or determine what ideas, of the many floating through her head, were relevant to what she was trying to do.

This was merely the beginning of an amygdala hijack, but as a professional, Dr. Peck saw that he was entering what was for him an uncharted danger zone, so be backed out, allowing Sarah to recover. In saving Sarah, he sadly failed to discover the power of the amygdala hijack.

Dr Peck wrote, "*I became frightened that I had made a mistake in confronting Sarah, as I listened to her lose control. Hartley* (her husband), *with his misery, his suicide attempts, and his pathetic existence, was bad enough; what could be served with both of them in the hospital? She probably felt cornered. I had better give her plenty of exit space so that she might pull herself together again.*"

He then ended his confrontation with her, and purposely gave her amygdala the ability to slow down its operations, at which point she recovered her amygdala function, and continued on as if nothing had happened. Sadly, Sarah used this respite to further cement her control over Hartley, whom she probably sent to an early grave. Had Dr Peck sent Sarah to the hospital, perhaps Hartley would have had a fighting chance to realize how nice life would have been without her.

I found the amygdala hijack to be an incredibly powerful technique when taken to completion, because when you use it, you are harnessing the narcissist's easily triggered amygdala to actually shut off a part of their brain that is critical to their brain's operations. I used the very force in their brain, which is strong enough to drive the narcissist to adhere to a false reality, against them. It's potency was no less powerful simply due to being wielded purposely by an individual of a rational mind.

Most amusingly, I acquired many of these techniques by watching narcissists use them on each other, as well as on innocent victims. Narcissists, perhaps due to the heightened sensitivity of their own amygdala's weaknesses, understand innately how to trigger the amygdalae of other people, and my experience is, they do it at every opportunity. If you know a narcissist, they have used at least some of these techniques on you at some point, whether consciously or unconsciously, to drive you to madness.

My impulse is to tell you to hijack your narcissist at every opportunity. Given how the narcissist targets your amygdala for attack, it is only fair that you should understand what they are doing, and use the same techniques on them. However, in this book I will advise against using these techniques on your narcissist, however tempting it may be.

In the following chapters we will discuss a full analysis of all the amygdala hijacking stimuli I have found useful myself, or observed others using. However, it should be noted that the amygdala hijack is kind of like a nuclear bomb. Set it off too close to you, and while you will destroy your enemy, you will also endure adverse consequences yourself. In the case of the amygdala hijack, if you use it on a narcissist with whom you are in close, regular proximity, several things will happen. First, your narcissist will become more agitated. It is kind of akin to hitting him with a hammer. It will hurt him, he will know you did it, and though he may never acknowledge that anything happened openly, he will hold it against you, and likely seek some form of revenge against you at a future date. For that reason alone, I advise against using these techniques, and emphasize that they are presented wholly to help you better understand how your narcissist is attacking you emotionally.

Second, I am not sure that you will not make your narcissist's narcissism worse when they are around you. You will literally be conditioning their already hair-trigger amygdala to fire off even more readily around you. My narcissist didn't show any clear symptoms of long term effects, but he may have gotten slightly worse after the hijacks – I really couldn't tell. Our relationship was already rapidly deteriorating, and a lot of other stuff was going wrong in his life, so it is tough to say whether his deterioration was due to the hijacks, or other circumstances. However it would be prudent to assume that you will make your narcissist worse around you in the long run.

Finally, you will amp up your narcissist's baseline amygdala activity, which may make them rage more. I am reminded of a phrase from a TV show, where one character said to another, of pranks they were pulling on a third, *"You're putting excess stress on a psychological structure that wasn't up to code to begin with."*

In short you could easily make your narcissist much, much worse. If you are trapped with your narcissist, it will give you a measure of power over them. But they could snap, deciding that this amygdala stimulation is untenable, and the only way out is to kill you. If you work with a narcissist, this technique could be a good way to make sure they leave you alone. It could even make them quit their job, due to a total inability to face you. But it could also push them over the edge, and they could come back to work with a bottle of cheap scotch and an AK-47, and begin shooting. There is no reliable way to predict what will happen.

For that reason, the following information, recounting the methods of amygdala hijacking that I have observed, as well as the specific ones that I used to bring my narcissist to his knees, is presented for informational purposes only. These methods are presented here only to give you a deeper understanding of how your narcissist thinks, and how they act out against you. Hopefully if you understand these techniques, you can armor yourself against the attacks of your narcissist, and defuse these techniques before they are able to have their effect on you.

I do not encourage you to use these techniques to hurt your narcissist, or try to drive them away from you. Although this worked quite well for me, it is my belief that I was probably lucky, and you might not enjoy such luck. You are warned.

Now, why are amygdala hijacks so painful?

Chapter Eight

What is the Amygdala Hijack?

Narcissists behave so strangely, because their amygdalae are uniquely wired to focus on negative stimuli, and experience an extraordinarily painful panic response in the face of it. All of the narcissist's strange behaviors are attempts to attenuate this painful panic response. When they deny reality, they are trying to tell themselves that the reality which pained them never happened, so they can disregard it, and shut off the production of the pain it produces.

When they explode at you specifically for noting some fact, it is because they see that fact as somehow negative, and they need you to stop drawing their attention to it (and activating their amygdala), so they can block it out of their mind (and take the pressure off their amygdala).

When they insist on being seen as superior to everyone else, they are attempting to short-circuit any honest measurement of their own worth, which might yield a negative piece of information about themselves – negative information which would freak them out to a degree that you can't imagine. Similarly, when they somehow degrade your enjoyment of life, it is because your happiness is reminding them of how unhappy they are, and triggering that panic response yet again. Every unusual behavior of the narcissist is an attempt to mechanically hack their own brain, and block out some aspect of reality which is paining it, and thereby amping up their amygdala. From issues of control and manipulation, to false realities, it all has this same basic root.

In short, the narcissist is attempting to shut off a neurological pain, which, if allowed to continue, will savage them mentally and even physically. But what kind of pain is this? How can it be so severe?

Deceased CBS newsman Mike Wallace appeared to describe this pain, when he described the effect of being criticized in the course of a lawsuit, by the lawyer for a man suing him. That mere verbal criticism, in court, caused him such mental pain that he physically collapsed in the courtroom, was rushed to the emergency room, and required several days of hospitalization before he could again function on his own. It subsequently sent him into a deep depression requiring extensive medical intervention to palliate.

In one interview about this, Wallace said, *"Well, I had to sit there in that drafty courtroom in Foley Square and the plaintiff put on its case first. So, I had to sit there every day and listen to myself publicly being called, in effect, a liar, a cheat and many other words to attack one's ethics and self-pride...At first I couldn't sleep, then I couldn't eat. I felt hopeless and I just couldn't cope... and then I just lost all perspective on things. You know, you become crazy...Finally, I collapsed and just went to bed."*[1]

In another interview he said, *"To be called "liar, cheat, fraud," et cetera, and in a libel case nothing is barred, little by little by little, I found myself getting spacey, and unable to sleep and unable to eat, and I mean really, what in the dickens is going on? ... I mean, it really was a tough one. I was copeless; not just hopeless, but copeless."*[2]

From another article describing a talk with Wallace, *"You sit there for the first two months and hear yourself called a liar and a cheat day after day, and you begin to feel lower than a snake's belly," "...the mental symptoms were even worse than the physical symptoms...and included the inability to concentrate, to remember what he read or to hear what he was being told."*[3] There are two interesting insights there. One, there were lasting physical symptoms after the initial collapse and hospitalization, which were quite bad themselves. The second insight is that concentration, focus, and motivation are all amygdala-intensive functions. If your amygdala has been savaged, to the point that it can now barely function (or you consciously or unconsciously hack the brain to try and turn it off), a loss of the ability to focus, and a loss of the force

[1] CBS Cares. (2011). "Information on Depression." <http://www.cbs.com/cbs_cares/topics/show/77488> (Accessed 20 May, 2014).

[2] "Mike Wallace Interview – Academy of Achievement" <http://www.achievement.org/autodoc/printmember/wal2int-1>

[3] Scarupa, H. (1991). "Lower than snake's belly' is how depression made Mike Wallace feel." <http://articles.baltimoresun.com/1991-04-18/features/1991108035_1_mike-wallace-depression-johns-hopkins> (Accessed 20 May, 2014).

in your brain which motivates action (something the amygdala does by focusing you on consequences, ie. *"I need to get this done or I will lose my job"*), would both be expected.

All of this occurred in response to merely hearing verbal criticism, in an environment in which verbal criticism was to be expected.[1] I have found, in my experiences with narcissists, that this trait, and this vulnerability, is quite common among them. I believe it is integrally related to the fundamental origin of their entire malady.

In another case seemingly describing an amygdala hijack, MIT Biology Professor Nancy Hopkins was listening to Harvard President Larry Summers speak. In the speech, Summers asserted that it might be possible that for evolutionary reasons, that female brains would have different aptitudes compared to male brains, and that this might lead

---

[1] It is interesting to note that in another interview, Mike Wallace stated to an interviewer that he had never experienced anything as depressing or emotionally affecting as hearing himself being castigated in that lawsuit. He had, by that time, traveled to where his missing son had last been seen on vacation, retraced his son's footsteps, and then discovered his own son's dead body at the foot of a cliff that his son had fallen off of. To Mike Wallace, the shock of discovering his own son's dead body was nothing, compared to the trauma of the amygdala hijack. It is worth noting that amygdala hijacks are most effective when executed with personally negative information. Negative information relevant to others will not have nearly as powerful an effect.

When the interviewer followed up, and asked if discovering his dead son's body had any similar type of traumatic effect on him, Wallace stated that, *"It was of course very, very painful. It also changed my life because it changed my career life. Before Peter's death, I was doing a variety of things in broadcasting. Not just news, because in those days you could do news, a quiz show and even commercials, and I did all of them. I used to say to myself, "Hey, you can't afford not to do some of these things in order to support your children." I had two of my own children then and two step-kids. When Peter was killed, I made up my mind... I was going to quit everything. I had enough money for a year. And it helped me cope by channeling some of this into my career choice: saying to myself "better do just what I want to do" and that meant getting a job exclusively in news."*

He then abandoned his wife and three remaining children, to pursue his own dreams.

From : CBS Cares. (2011). "Information on Depression." <http://www.cbs.com/cbs_cares/topics/show/77488> (Accessed 20 May, 2014).

females and males to seek out different occupational specialties. This material conflicted with Hopkin's apparent intellectual devotion to sexual equalitarianism, and as a result, in Hopkin's own words, *"I felt I was going to be sick. My heart was pounding and my breath was shallow. I was extremely upset. I just couldn't breath because this type of bias makes me physically ill."* She went on to say that had she not immediately fled the speech, *"I would have either blacked out or thrown up."*

In another case, author Matt Forney[1] wrote an article about why excessive female self esteem could be bad for women on his blog.[2] A feminist blogger immediately posted the article to her friends,[3] after only cursorily glancing at it. After posting it, she tried to read it a little deeper, and then added to following warnings to her post, for any feminists who happened on her site and were tempted to read Matt's article.

"EDIT: GUYS PLEASE BE CAREFUL READING THIS BECAUSE I THINK I'M STARTING TO GET A BLACKOUT FROM SHEER ANGER AND I'M ONLY ON HIS FIRST "REASON"

"EDIT 2: HEY, FOR YOUR OWN SAFETY, SINCE I HAVE NO IDEA WHAT TO TAG THIS AS, PLEASE JUST... TRY NOT TO READ THAT OK? HE STARTS TALKING ABOUT STUFF LIKE... DEPRESSION AND SELF-HARM AND HOW THAT.... IS A RESULT OF BEING A CONFIDENT GIRL AND STUFF... AND HOW ANTIDEPRESSANTS ARE A SUBSTITUTE FOR "A MAN'S LOVING EMBRACE" AND IT TOOK ME 10 MINUTES TO TYPE THIS BECAUSE I'M DIZZY AND HARDLY BREATHING AND I'M HAVING A BLACKOUT."

I read these, and I see how easily they could be conditioned. I see Bob, sitting in that little desk after the recess free-for-all, his brain burning into itself all of the neural pathways to produce this type of response, as his vision begins to deteriorate, his heart pounds, his

---

[1]   "Matt Forney's Home Page." <http://www.mattforney.com> (Accessed 20 May 2014).

[2]   Forney, M. (2013) "The case against female self-esteem." <http://mattforney.com/2013/09/16/the-case-against-female-self-esteem/> (Accessed 20 May, 2014).

[3]   Author Unknown. (2013) "Untitled post." <http://cantankerouscrab.tumblr.com/post/63922084887/spookstageleft-scarlettingridjo-i-need> (Accessed 20 May, 2014).

stomach churns, and the sensations of nausea grow toward a full on vomit-thon. (Even as I contemplate all of those symptoms, I wonder what other symptoms Bob had, that he didn't make the mistake of telling me about.)

To be clear, I have no idea of the clinical diagnosis for any of the above people. However I am quite certain that those physical symptoms that they are describing, in response to encountering mere ideas, are identical to the very physical force which your narcissist is running from on a regular basis. Every crazy action they take, every rage they throw, and every reality they deny – they are all programmed behaviors that the narcissist is conditioned to engage in, to try and spare them from experiencing the symptoms and effects described above. You cannot understand the narcissistic mind without picturing yourself, living your life at the mercy of a force such as that, seemingly triggered randomly by circumstances you can't even focus well enough on, to avoid reliably. A force which unleashes a pain in your brain that is so severe, you will vomit, blackout, rage, and even require physical hospitalization to recover from.

What we will be doing with the amygdala hijack, is figuring out what triggers this pain, as well as how the narcissist modifies their thinking and behavior to try to ameliorate the sensation. To give you a deeper understanding of the narcissist's mind, I will describe the methods I used to innocently present these stimuli to the narcissist, precipitate the negative sensations, and prevent their attenuation by the narcissist so as to maximize their cognitive effects.

The narcissist has spent their entire life practicing keeping this sensation at bay. They have grown accustomed to controlling it in the moderate doses in which it normally presents itself (doses so small that we do not even notice them in our lives). What they are not accustomed to is having this sensation actively called up and elicited purposefully and consistently, for a sustained period, by an individual who understands it fully.

Even employing the incredible array of bizarre and extreme behaviors and perceptual modifications that narcissists use, even when actually arriving at the point where they are denying the very reality around them, the narcissist is still horribly afflicted by emotional pain and panic, simply in the face of the basic rigors of going about their day.

Once I figured out how to trigger their panic and pain purposefully, to prevent them from attenuating the effects, and began eliciting it strongly for sustained periods, I was able to literally use my narcissist's mental weakness to short circuit his own brain.

If you can reach the point where you understand how I did this, you will have a phenomenal understanding of your narcissist's mind that will rival any professional's.

Chapter Nine

Amygdala Hijacking Techniques

Here we will delve into how the amygdala hijack is engendered by narcissists, as well as how I engendered it with my narcissist. This is all based upon my personal experiences triggering hijacks, and my observations of others. As such, it may be incomplete, or even incorrect in places. Unfortunately, I am aware of no other work on this subject to use as a foundation. Until there is a suitable body of research and experience to draw upon, the following will have to do.

Before we start – a word of caution. If you hijack your narcissist, you are upping the stakes in the relationship. Your narcissist will likely grow desperate emotionally. First, as you hijack them, they may begin to neurologically develop the ability to experience the panic which drives their disorder more potently, and that panic will come ever easier to them. You may, in essence, be exercising the *"panic muscle"* in their brain, and like a muscle, it may grow larger and stronger. Their condition, and all the traits which accompany it – uncontrolled rages, depressing behavioral traits, insistence on false realities, and even violent acting out to assert control, may grow worse. They may need you to be ever more miserable to reclaim any semblance of emotional normalcy for themselves.

The narcissist is unstable, and unable to control their behavior to begin with. Begin hacking into their brain to repeatedly trigger the very panicked pain response which makes them act irrationally to begin with, and you may snap something inside of them, and produce unpredictable effects. For that reason, this section of the book will be for informational purposes only. If you disregard this instruction and employ these techniques to hijack your narcissist, be vigilant, and stay alert to any signs of danger. Your life might just depend upon it. As we say in this book, if you are here, you are likely dealing with the worst form of narcissist. Do not underestimate them.

Before we begin, some clarification. An amygdala hijack is actually likely a hyper-activation of specific emotion/discomfort-producing regions of the Anterior Cingulate Cortex or possibly even other parts of the brain, by an amygdala that both focuses on a negative stimulus, and is unable to find a cognitive path to eliminate the stimulus from the environment, or reduce its perceived importance.

The term *"neural hijack"* was first used by author Daniel Goleman in the book *Emotional Intelligence: Why It Can Matter More Than IQ.*[1] He described such a hijack taking over the amygdala. Since then, the term *"amygdala hijack"* has become a popularized term, so this work will continue its use. The pain which is produced by an amygdala hijack is similar to fear or panic, though I suspect, based on experience with narcissists, that it is more primal, visceral, and perhaps physical in nature in narcissists. Called Aversive Stimulus in the field, it is, in reality, probably produced in response to the activation of specific areas of the Anterior Cingulate Cortex by an amygdala that has flagged as significant, some negative stimulus, and which has issued a call to the ACC to produce the required aversive stimulus.

Since the term *"amygdala hijack"* was already coined to describe this effect, this text will continue to use that terminology and refer to the amygdala exclusively as the organ involved, for simplicity. So, for example, this book will say that, *"this will stimulate the amygdala,"* or *"the amygdala will produce panic."* However what is actually occurring is a more complex mechanism, involving using the amygdala to call up panic from another organ, while preventing the amygdala from focusing on any stimuli which might allow it to disregard the hijacking stimulus. So although this book will speak of the amygdala creating the pain of the hijack, in reality, the amygdala is calling for the production of that pain by another organ.

This book is not a text on neuroscience, nor would our readers need these issues overcomplicated, even if the science in these areas were clearly resolved and conclusive. So although the following sections will say amygdala, those interested in a fuller understanding, who will do their own further research, should know that this is certainly a gross simplification. Conversely, those interested in merely exerting control over their narcissist should simply assume that all they are doing is

---

[1]   Goleman, Daniel. (1996). *Emotional Intelligence: Why It Can Matter More Than IQ.* New York City, NY: Bantam Books.

stimulating the amygdala, which causes an unbearable pain in the brain of their narcissist.

We cannot imagine this force, because it does not rule us. Within our brains, the stimulus produced by the amygdala is tolerable under all but the most extreme circumstances. Even so, we ourselves have our breaking points. Placed under enough stress, almost anyone could become afflicted with some form of amygdala dysfunction, ranging from sensations of extreme panic, to full blown Post Traumatic Stress Disorder.

One thing you may notice is that these stresses that we will describe here, as triggering this effect, will seem inconsequential to you. I noticed the same thing, and I suspect it is why this has never been postulated or examined before.

For some time I never even attempted to use these techniques for that reason, even though I had been noticing them being used repeatedly by the narcissists I knew. I viewed them as petty, cheap, and at most, a minor irritation. I always felt that when I was angry enough to strike, I would use a physical deathblow, not what appeared to me to be the emotional equivalent of a mosquito bite. For that reason, I thought these types of attacks were below me, and not worth my time or energy. Though I cataloged how the narcissists around me used these, I never thought about using them myself. For me, identifying all of these techniques was an exercise in cataloging the many variations of the narcissist's patheity and weakness. These were the impotent techniques of cowards and losers, resorted to when desperation and resignation combined to dictate that one had no more powerful option.

That changed one day, when frustrated by my narcissist, I found myself unable to respond violently, yet angry enough at what he had done to another that I really wanted to. Out of frustration, and a lack of other viable legal options, I decided to put on an unemotional countenance, and do to him what he did to others. I employed these techniques, and was astonished at the panic, horror, rage, and finally outright physical illness that I easily created.

Within several minutes, I was driving him to the emergency room for what I believed was a stroke that he had suffered coincidentally, that was unrelated to the hijack. Only later, after doctors proclaimed their mystification about his symptoms, did I realize that the "stroke" had been engendered by these techniques. I subsequently repeated the phenomenon again and again, to the point that the narcissist in question began to not even go to the hospital, choosing to simply lie down until the symptoms passed. Since discussing this online, several people have written to me, telling me that they have done the same thing to narcissists that they knew, and that the symptoms they engendered were no less severe.

Narcissists are so bizarre because they literally have to be. Let reality truly touch them, even in just a casual glance, and the extent of the physical symptoms they will experience would blow your mind. Discovering the true extent of this Achilles heel is a vital step in understanding the true depths of their mental illness, and the lengths they can feel compelled to resort to, in acting out against you.

Finally, this information on the amygdala hijack should serve two purposes for you, the reader. Firstly, it will explain to you exactly what your narcissist is - and why. Understand these techniques, and you will begin to fully understand your narcissist's evil, their inability to control it, and your need to get as far away as possible. Secondly, and just as importantly, it offers you a detailed view of your narcissist's arsenal, and the weapons they are using on you. If you understand what the narcissist is doing, it diminishes the effects of it, and can begin to armor you against their attacks.

There are two primary means by which to stimulate an amygdala that will be discussed in the coming chapters. There may be more which will come to the fore as this study continues, but to date, I have only identified two. The two means are conceptual and physical/mechanical.

Chapter Ten

The Conceptual Amygdala Hijack_____

We will first deal with the conceptual means by which to trigger the amygdala. This is the most complex method by which to stimulate amygdalae, since it relies on the use of complex thought, rather than simple means such as specific physical/mechanical actions. I do not know if this is more powerful, due to complex thought being more exhausting to the brain, or less powerful, due the the complex thought required to trigger it, diluting the activation of the amygdalae, which is itself a more primitive organ, naturally responsive to deeper, more primitive stimuli. I will state that the most powerful amygdala hijack that I ever did was almost fully conceptual, and it produced the full "stroke."

I have also noted previously that writer Matt Forney has written several pieces which functioned solely as conceptual amygdala hijacks, only to see feminists repost his material on feminist sites, while complaining that the pieces gave them symptoms of amygdala hijacks, such as blackouts and the inability to breathe. (You know your Gung Fu is strong when you write mere words on a computer screen, and your enemies spontaneously vomit and black out inside their own homes, when they read them.)

To review quickly, before discussing the conceptual hijack, the amygdala flags specific items for significance, focuses the mind on them, and calls for a brain shock, technically called *"Aversive Stimulus,"* likely by triggering the Anterior Cingulate Cortex, which is what actually delivers the shock. The amygdala triggers this shock strongly when it deems a significant stimulus to be negative.

Two primary factors appear to combine with one complex factor, all of which then combine with two minor factors, to determine the size of the shock delivered, and the extent of the amygdala/ACC activation.

The two primary factors will be self-relevance, and degree of negativity. This is simple, since a highly self-relevant stimulus, which is highly negative, will deliver a greater amygdala-stimulating/ACC-triggering effect than a non-self-relevant stimulus which is deemed only slightly negative. As an example, a weak criticism of a stranger is, to a narcissist, weak in both relevance, and negativity, and thus will produce a weak aversive stimulus response. By contrast, a strong criticism of your target, in a way they instinctually care about being criticized, will be high in both relevance and negativity to your target, and that will maximize the aversive stimulus produced.

A third, complex factor, will be correctness of the stimulus. It is obvious that a highly self-relevant stimulus, which is deemed enormously negative will exert less of an effect, if it can easily be shown to be incorrect. Here, the nature of its incorrectness will diminish it's relevance, and that will diminish the extent of the hijack. However, a highly self-relevant stimulus, which is deemed enormously negative, will exert more of an effect, if it is incorrect, but it cannot be shown to be incorrect, and the observing crowd is left believing it to be true. Here, the incorrect status will draw the amygdala's attention even more, trigger the error-monitoring function of the ACC even more,[1] and result in even greater aversive stimulus, despite the precipitating stimulus being no more relevant or negative. Imagine being imprisoned because you were correctly blamed for a murder you enjoyed commuting. Now imagine being imprisoned similarly, but because an enemy lied, and said you had committed it when you had not. That would be an increased aversive stimulus.

I suspect that the additional activation of the ACC's error-monitoring, as well as perhaps a perception of unfairness, may increase

---

[1]   The ACC is a very complex organ, issuing a neural alarm when encountering a variety of stimuli. Although it will issue a neural alarm at the amygdala's behest, it can also issue an alarm on its own, usually due to some detection of an error in the data it is analyzing. Here, our primary concern is analyzing how to combine its amygdala-precipitated alarm, with its self-motivated issuing of a neural alarm when encountering a variety of stimuli, including, but not limited to, error-detections, envy of others, physical pain, incongruence of data (such as the word "red" written in blue letters), unfairness, or social ostracization from a group. Here, in this example, we are combining a call for alarm due to amygdala activation with a call for alarm due to error detection (and possibly unfairness), in an attempt to magnify the scale of the ultimate alarm issued.

the aversive stimulus it will produce, when triggered by the amygdala. It is already known that if your amygdala is activated by one stimulus, (such as a need to focus, or the stress of a pending task), you can be more prone to see minor stimuli trip your amygdala, and precipitate an angry outburst. You may even remember apologizing once, for just such an incident, saying something along the lines of, *"I'm sorry, it's just I've got this job hanging over me, and I've been so stressed...,"* in response to snapping at someone over something which, viewed logically, was too minor (ie. shouldn't have been flagged by the amygdala) to have warranted the outburst.

I suspect that the ACC works similarly, and if you can load it not just with an initial negative "neural-alarm"-precipitating-stimulus, but also trip it's unfairness, expectation-violation, or error-monitoring functions, it will amplify the output of the subsequent alarm produced. The key is to flag the error-monitoring function, without allowing the error to in any way diminish the practical relevance of the triggering stimulus to the amygdala.

I also know that the narcissists I have known have seemed to relish breaking rules, and I think that a knowledge of the heightening-effect that perceptions of unfairness/error-monitoring/expectation-violations have on ACC activation, may explain why they have relished such rule-breaking so much. If what they do is bad, and you know it is unfair but can do nothing about it, they know it is even more affecting, in the way they seek to affect, than had they adhered to "rules."[1] I see the modern Liberal, written all over that.

I first noticed this quality of the ACC/amygdala relationship in a narcissist who insisted on asserting factually incorrect material, and refusing to deny that it was incorrect when challenged. In fact, when challenged, he asserted it even more strongly, even in the face of logical arguments which should have convinced him of his error. Those who dealt with him found arguing with him exhausting, and I now believe he was doing this purposefully, to further stimulate the aversive stimulus produced in those he dealt with. I will confess, before coming to

---

[1]   Rules here can be morals, standard of decency, etc, and the means by which they are violated could involve technical rule adherence, such as following the letter of a law to an unfair or immoral outcome. The main idea is that doing something unfair, be it cheating, or attaining an immoral result. Rule violations also serve as expectation violations, as we will discuss later.

understand his malady, I went back and forth with him several times myself, and ended up exhausted and irritated, probably to his great amusement. Although I am not positive that the cognitive mechanism is correct, it would make sense. The ACC does appear to deliver the panic and shock produced by a negative stimulus, on the amygdala's request, and it is possible that purposely introducing an error/unfairness/expectation-violation-stimulus as well, to further activate the ACC, would enhance the shock it delivers.

Another example would be to visualize the person who is sick, but can't find a diagnosis. Doctors tell them they are well, but the lingering uncertainty is highly stressful. Give them a firm diagnosis, and now they know they are sick, and have a concrete piece of negative information, but they report feeling happier that they at least know the truth. There, certainty is diminishing the degree of aversive stimulus produced by a negative piece of information. Thus uncertainty itself can be amygdala-stimulating due to it's introduction of a feeling of potential loss of control, and the risk inherent in that. Uncertainty can also be frustrating, as the medical example would demonstrate, and frustration is amygdala stimulating.

Additionally, uncertainty can provoke further thought, and further examination of a stimulus by the amygdala, all of which will further focus the target's amygdala on the original stimulus concept. If the concept is amygdala stimulating to begin with, uncertainty, combined with plausibility, can be further amygdala stimulating, as the target is focused on the idea by the uncertainty of the stimulus and the natural desire to correctly resolve its verifiable status.

As an example of how certainty can erode the effectiveness of an amygdala hijack by diminishing focus, imagine presenting to a narcissist you know, a devastating, fully-certain fact which, if accepted, would savage his amygdala. His immediate reflexive response will be total denial - a mental blockage to allowing the idea into his consciousness. This blockage will provide a relief to his amygdala, as he ensconces himself within his false reality. For this reason, the certainty of a stimulus does not have a consistent effect on the degree to which an amygdala hijack is effective on a narcissist.

I have found that Liberal political ideologues argue more, and seem to get more worked up, over issues, that while overwhelmingly negative, offer some small degree of uncertainty, or argue-ability. By contrast, the idea of politics as r/K Selection Theory, which all Liberals seem to immediately see as unarguable when presented it, seems to drive them into a shell, causing them to reflexively disengage, refuse to discuss it, deny that they ever even heard of the concept, and demand that others cease talking about it. Bear in mind, that the amygdala hijack is about stimulating the amygdala more than winning an argument. As a result, there will be some circumstances where introducing a little uncertainty can be your friend.

So here, correctness will be termed a complex stimulus. Incorrectness can either turn off the aversive stimulus triggered by the amygdala, if it can be used to diminish the relevance of a stimulus, or turn it on even more, if it is known, but not able to be used to diminish the relevance. Likewise, correctness can either heighten the aversive stimulus produced by a negative stimulus by increasing its relevance, or reduce it by either diminishing ACC activation, or precipitating a denial mechanism, plunging the individual deeper into their false reality.

There is a fourth minor factor, external to the actual conceptual hijack, which can affect the relative power of the hijack, and it appears to be the perceived emotional state of the hijacker. A highly emotional hijacker can divert the amygdala focus of the target from the hijacking stimulus. We will discuss this emotional-state-factor more as part of the subsequent examination of mechanical hijacks, which are designed to amplify conceptual hijacks using more primitive amygdala triggers.

Finally, one last minor factor is the cumulative nature of the hijacking. The amygdala is like a muscle. Each time it is used, it expends its energy reserves, and as it exhausts itself it becomes less able to handle subsequent stimulations. I have noted that my main narcissist seemed to know this, and would focus himself on providing amygdala stimulant after amygdala stimulant to his targets, sometimes displaying an expression which just faintly betrayed an eager expectancy, as his target grew increasingly agitated, and ever closer to an emotional hijack. In retrospect, he was waiting for an outcome that he knew was approaching.

So bear in mind that when I would pursue an amygdala hijack, I would rarely deliver a single hijacking stimulus, and then sit back gleefully, as I watched my target melt down mentally and emotionally.

Rather, I needed to load their amygdala cumulatively, with an understanding that each hijacking stimulus would take a little out of their amygdala's gas tank, and bring them a little closer to that point where their amygdala couldn't possibly handle even a single iota of additional stress. Once I reached that point, I would literally force their brain into a shutdown by providing that last bit of fully-overloading amygdala stimulation.

In Narcissists in particular, this can be a difficult concept to grasp, because their initial countenance will be one of self-assurance and bluster, and that will progress rapidly when challenged, to rage and an extreme assertion of control. Know that they are doing that out of desperation. Understand that their facade hides a fragile ego that is easily shattered, and a brain which often begins aggressive encounters at the edge of it's operational envelope. Don't be deceived by the eagerness with which they will rage – it is desperation, and just beyond that rage can be a mental breakdown which, when witnessed, appears more a failure of the physical brain structures required to run their mind and body, than any mere emotional breakdown.

Now when structuring a conceptual hijack, I would know all about my target's beliefs, and how they were using those beliefs to calm their own anxiety. Conceptual hijacks should be customized to whatever extent possible. Feminists, and those men who think feminism stupid, can read the same concepts and themes, and have vastly different cognitive responses. Tell a feminist that women are emotionally weak, illogical, and unfit for leadership, and you will provoke a different cognitive response in their amygdala than you would see if you presented the same concept to a member of the anti-feminist-manosphere. Know your enemy.

In my experience there are several themes I have seen archetypical narcissists respond very strongly to. All of these themes, to one degree or another, are realities that the narcissist is trying to deny, to assuage their own insecurities. Most can be easily identified by the immediate rage that their assertion will trigger, or by the narcissist's use of them to try and irritate those around them.

Below you will find some of the conceptual themes I have made note of. These are mostly generalized stimuli, or ones which worked well on my narcissists. In general however, hijacking stimuli will be specific and customized to specific narcissists, since different narcissists will have different insecurities, and different amygdala-sensitivities, often rooted in different developmental and childhood experiences.

If one wishes to try and imagine what customized themes might yield effective hijacks on their own narcissist, they should make note of the fact that narcissists project their own psychologies on everyone around them. Many of the things a narcissist will say to irritate you, were first thought of by the narcissist because they are the things which would have struck a deathblow to the narcissist themselves, had you delivered them in kind. Observe what they say closely. See if some of the accusations they make, the assertions they present, or the ideas they bring up, are concepts which the narcissist themselves would explode at, if your roles were reversed, and you raised them yourself. If so, you have a customized theme. However, I will reiterate, I do not recommend using these techniques for anything more than as an intellectual exercise designed to help you better understand your narcissist, and the forces precipitating his unusual behavioral drives.

I'm the Good One

The first conceptual theme we will examine is one which produces a narcissist behavior sometimes referred to as *Reinforcing the Narcissistic Bubble*. If you know a narcissist, you've seen this one. You begin calm and happy. They start an argument, press any button in you which they can find, escalate it to screaming if possible, and then, just as you reach the pinnacle of agitation, they suddenly calm down, look smug and self-assured, and point out how crazy you look as you yell at them. I call this theme, *I'm The Good One*, though some call it *Reinforcing the Narcissistic Bubble*.

When using this on narcissists, I found it best used after I had hijacked them as much as possible, and they were at maximal agitation. Just as the target reached maximal agitation, I would step back, and calmly ask why they are so out of control, as I looked at the crowd confusedly, (and a little worried about how weird the narcissist looked). This really drove the narcissists I used it on crazy, especially as I became hyper-calm and logical.

This can also be used defensively. If a narcissist was beginning to irritate me, I would first command them to relax, or calm down (said either as if their weirdness or agitation was bothering me, or with a look of genuine concern for their well-being). They will immediately, emphatically respond that they are relaxed (almost as if they are insulted that you would imply they weren't). That shift in their amygdala's focus would usually lead them to cease their attempt to agitate.

The assertion, implying that they are somehow in an aberrant mental state, will trip their panic response at the thought of their own aberrant nature being revealed, and force them to assume a hyper-relaxed, more manageable, and more tolerable countenance. So if your narcissist is being irritating in any way, assume a more relaxed state, and command them to calm down, or stop getting so worked up. Portray them as a little crazy, and yourself as a little unnerved by their craziness, as you observe them calmly.

This accusation of agitation will be even more demotivating to them if they aren't worked up when you say it. They will try to debate you, to which you should seriously tell them that they are not even aware of how anxious they look, and how worked up they seem. Look concerned for their well-being. Again, incorrectness and uncertainty can both add to the effect here, as the narcissist, who is naturally anxious, and prone to define reality based on the beliefs of others, may wonder if they are failing to hide their baseline state, or whether you are lying just to irritate them. Although this is not a real hijack when used in such a fashion (it is more of a distracting/demotivating technique, than a panic-inducer), it can be an immensely useful, and easy-to-apply manipulation of the narcissist's psychology.

Competitive/Relative Inferiority

This concept is a general one which I have seen used any number of ways. Narcissists are weirdly competitive and strangely envious over seemingly insignificant details, from how the salary they earn compares to other's, to the respectability of the shampoo they use, compared to the shampoos that others use. It is a shielding mechanism, designed to protect their ego, and their amygdala, from confronting their own insecurity.

You can sometimes spot this trait in a narcissist, by how they will try to verbally downplay their competitiveness in realms where they can't compete, as a way of creating a false reality where they don't care about their competitive inferiority. If your narcissist, out of the blue says, *"Other people are obsessed with how much money they earn, but I really don't care about things like that,"* then you know they were just obsessing over exactly that subject. They are trying to establish a verbalized reality where their not caring, will allow their brain to relax over their abject failure in that regard. My own narcissist actually made this statement once, and then later went about trying to hijack a relative over their relative inferiority, on a money-related issue. In reality my favorite narcissist's low income level was one of his greatest vulnerabilities. (This is one of the reasons that a narcissist's verbalizations are often 180 degrees counter to reality. They are not just trying to deceive you. They are trying to deceive themselves – to verbally define their own reality in such a way as to assuage their own amygdala discomfort. If they say they are superior, and you don't immediately point out how they are not, they can tell themselves they are, because you believe it too.)

For this reason, I found that focusing a narcissist on someone else's greatness and success, and making them examine their own relative failure at the same time, was enormously amygdala stimulating. One key I found was to figure out a way to revisit the topic from different angles, so as to maintain the target's focus on the inferiority for a sustained period. The narcissist is designed to touch on such inferiority, and then rapidly deny it and block it from their consciousness. I would innocently bring it up, marvel at it, ask if was inferior in one way, act shocked that it was, inquire if the inferiority was another way, shake my head sorrowfully at its scope, see if the inferiority extended to another perspective, and then I would laugh at the sheer magnitude of it, its dis-believable nature, the degree to which it could never be surmounted, and so on. It was through maintaining the focus on it that their amygdala depleted its reserves, and began to become unable to maintain a relaxed and functional state.

When hijacking, each hijack takes a little out of their amygdala's gas tank. I always viewed my goal as being to rev their amygdala up, and burn through all of those reserves as quickly as possible.

The Inevitability of Failure Has Already Occurred

Narcissists personalize failure. To a normal person, failure can occur to anyone, and it does not mean the individual is a failure. Failure is a normal part of the process of experience, which eventually leads to mastery, and which eventually produces success. Indeed, a normal person will view the willingness to fail in pursuit of greatness as doggedness and determination - very positive traits.

However to the narcissist, failure speaks to who they are fundamentally – they are either a success, or a failure. Incapable of perceiving any other objective logical metric, and desperate for any tangible refutation of their own deep sense of personal inferiority, to a narcissist success or failure is the sole determinant of an individual's worth and value. This is in part probably due to part of their problem being an easily overwhelmed amygdala which, if not deluded with false reality, will detect any hint of negativity and then artificially amplify its relevance, and shock them commensurately with aversive stimulus. To a narcissist, if they fail, and they can't deny the failure somehow, then that stimulus is immediately flagged as vitally, singularly important, focused upon, and their logical response to this is aversive stimulus.

In presenting this stimulus, I found that it was important to understand that the narcissist's brain is constantly on the lookout for cognitive band-aids, designed to modify the perception of hijacking stimuli, and make them less noxious. One such band-aid applicable here was to tell themselves that the failure hadn't happened yet, and thus was not inevitable. For this reason, I found it best to always present this hijack in the present tense, emphasizing that the failure had already occurred. Presenting it as a failure that was going to happen in the future, did not have as aggressive a hijacking effect, in my experience. Thus, if narcissist required "X" to happen to succeed, rather than emphasize solely that X wouldn't happen, I would emphasize that "X" was an event whose occurrence had already been prevented, and thus they had already failed, before even beginning.

I also found it important when I used this to identify only goals which were relevant to the narcissist, and which would be flagged by their amygdala as important, as well as forceful, factual demonstrations of their present failure, or the inevitable nature of their impending failure, making it into a present failure. Occasionally I would tie their own personal inferiority into the hijack, citing their inferiority as a causative source of their failure. Combined these would haunt the narcissist, by penetrating the bubble of fantasy they built around themselves, where they are perfect, and everything always would work out their way.

Diminution of Stature/Humiliation

This is a very powerful technique. The narcissist needs to feel as if they have power, so as to pacify their insecure amygdala. It is only when everyone around them reflexively supplicates, that the narcissist can let their amygdala relax. For this reason, narcissists often build a perception of themselves as superiors, and they demand that others treat them this way. If they are not treated this way, their amygdala will go on guard, and begin to activate. That activation by itself consumes resources, and it sets the stage for an even more resource-consumptive rage.

I found that diminution of stature or humiliation attacks can occur a number of ways. They can range from small slights, such as getting drinks for everyone but the narcissist (I would feign sorrow and remorse at forgetting them, to focus them on the fact that I forgot them – the anger still festered), to presenting a hypothetical example of something which portrays the narcissist as helpless and powerless, to insults in passing, denigrating the narcissist's skills, abilities, morals, intellect, etc. These techniques are very powerful because they wound the narcissist's false-self directly, so they would often provoke outbursts. For this reason, I found that they were best employed in conjunction with some technique designed to suppress conflict, and force the narcissist to bottle up their anger, as will be discussed later. (One example being following an insult with a quick change of subject. Changes of subject force the narcissist to return the conversation back to the denigration, and visit it again, or leave it be and let the insult stand. Often their amygdala will actually prevent them from drawing the conversation back, leading to much stifled anger as they repeatedly contemplate the negative information which was just entered into the group's "official record," but about which they can do nothing.)

Insist on Arguable Untruths

This is a technique some narcissists do, and it can be particularly frustrating. It is presented here only to provide a further window into the narcissist mind. I assume if you used this yourself, it could degrade your own reputation for honesty or intelligence.

Narcissists who do this will insist on an untruth, especially one which would impede the attainment of a goal important to the group, and then they will refuse to acknowledge the falsity of the untruth. I fully believe narcissists who practice this technique do it knowingly. They know that what they are asserting is false, they enjoy seeing you upset over the fact that they are so unable to accept logic, and they refuse to give in purposely, to watch you grow increasingly agitated and frustrated.

To these narcissists, truth is immaterial, the group's goals are meaningless, and your upset emotional state is blissfully amusing. As a result they have one goal – to see you frustrated. If they tell you the sky is pink, and you begin to get agitated asserting that it is blue, they will tell you it is pink again, and laugh to themselves as you get increasingly frustrated. If you are assigned to a team at work, and the narcissists insists on a piece of information which will cause your project to fail, you will get quite upset arguing with him. In that case, the very fact that his erroneous piece of data will cause you all to fail is probably why he targeted it specifically.

In theory, I assume this could be used against narcissists quite effectively, if one found a piece of information which, if believed by everyone, would cause them to see their false-self injured, or their narcissistic bubble of false reality blown up. In life, normal people have tangible goals and close personal relationships, but narcissists have only the false-self – that imaginary version of themselves in their head, which is perfect and awesome, and which shields their amygdala from the awful reality of their own patheity. Strangely, their false-self only seems to work effectively if they can get other people to believe in it.

If you combine a call to the ACC from the amygdala for alarm, due to a perceived insult to the false-self within the social-group, with a call for alarm for error-monitoring due to the information actually being false, with a third call for alarm due to frustration at not being able to invalidate the assertion, you will amplify the power rating of the hijack immensely. If you have suffered under the false slander of a narcissist, it is my belief that this is why narcissists will do this to you. If you have no morals, no sense of right and wrong (or reality for that matter), and are solely focused on stimulating your target's amygdala to call for an epic burst of aversive stimulus, this is the type of attack you launch.

I never used this one much, though, and I would encourage you to avoid it as well.

Privacy Invasion and Being a Central Information Hub

Two things narcissists try to do to irritate is to invade privacy, and control and guide the flow of all information. This is probably due to some deep perception that their entire self-worth is defined by the group's beliefs and perceptions (ie, it's acceptance of their false reality), combined with an assumption (erroneously assuming that everyone else thinks like them), that everyone else's self-worth is as well. Thus, to a narcissist, control the information flow, and you control everyone's self-assessments of their own self-worth. To the narcissist, that information is pure power over not just everyone, but in the narcissist's mind, the very (false) reality that everyone inhabits. For a Narcissist, control is the ultimate amygdala-relaxant.

In my experience these traits were easily exploitable as hijacking stimuli. If I were using them today I would accidentally expose things the narcissist wouldn't want known, and then feign ignorance over why the release of the information would upset them. I would intrude into their private spaces, and then feign ignorance of why they should care that I was there. I would acquire information I shouldn't have access to, and feign ignorance of why it should matter that I had it, or released it. If I got a juicy piece of information about someone that others would want to know, and the person wouldn't mind me sharing it, I would do so before the narcissist could release it themselves. To the narcissist, they should have free access to everyone else's information, nobody should have free, unfettered access to theirs, and they should be the one central hub who everyone looks to for any information. Much of this has to do with issues of control, especially control of everyone else's perceptions of reality. The narcissist wants everyone else to look to them, to define everybody's reality for them. The last thing the narcissist wants is everyone talking freely amongst themselves, and coming to their own conclusions.

Arrogance – I Have Succeeded, and You Have Failed

Normal people will tend to not expound on their own successes. If the goal was to be hijacking narcissists however, they should make an exception when around narcissists. Few things are as frustrating to a narcissist as someone else holding themselves out as superior, or worse, pointing to instances where the narcissist has failed, but where they have succeeded. I can still see Bob smoldering with rage when I did this to him once, only to finally explode at me for being, "...so *God-damned arrogant!*" I would smile benignly, with an expression that exuded repressed pleasure at people extolling my virtues, at moments like that.

If I wanted to do this, I would regale crowds with tales of my adventures and travels to exotic places, amaze everyone with accounts of my extensive accomplishments, demand special treatment beyond that which the narcissist received, and I would always treat the narcissist as an inferior. If possible, I would point out where the narcissist had failed where I had succeeded, and where they had fallen short of the mark I had always set for myself. Ideally this would all be done in front of the crowd. Most effective of all, I would always exude an aura of arrogance, entitlement, pleasure with myself, and inherent superiority, because this produces in the narcissist a constant slow burn of amygdala stimulation that nicely complements the acutely sharp pokes and jabs of other hijacking techniques.

As I did this, I would hold others in the narcissist's various fields of interest out as experts and sages, whose advice everyone should seek. I would recount their successes and accomplishments at length, and extensively laud their abilities and knowledge. I would totally focus the crowd's attentions on them.

One thing the narcissist uses against us is our innate drive to politeness. We would not do these things with friends. Even if we became aware that we had grossly outcompeted a friend in some arena, we would never raise the issue because we will go out of our way to make our friends feel happy. Introducing some competitive vibe to the relationship, by attempting to demonstrate where you have out-performed a friend would be crass, rude, and impolite. In more technical terms, it would risk stimulating your friend's amygdala, and friends don't stimulate their friends' amygdalae. We strive to see our friends in a place of happiness and pleasantness, and politeness is the tool by which we place them in it, through the amygdala-relaxing effect it has on them.

Narcissists are another story, however. As we have pointed out, narcissists ignore the normal goals and desires we hold sacrosanct. They have one overriding purpose which they have been trained to pursue from childhood – assuaging their amygdala – and this is often accomplished by stimulating the amygdalae of others. Growing up, whenever their focus has strayed from that purpose, their amygdala has trained them like a dog, yanking the chain of their ACC, applying aversive stimulus, and forcing them to fortify their false reality, support their false self, and try to render someone else, nearby, worse off.

By adulthood, they have one goal in life, and it is to desperately try to keep their amygdala from being activated. Be it a denial of reality, an embrace of fantasy, or just creating a world around them where everyone else is worse off and miserable, the narcissist is a single-minded machine in sole pursuit of this goal. Arrogance fits all bills, fortifying their false reality, denying their reality, and irritating everyone around them.

I suspect arrogance in the people around them irritates narcissists most of all, because of the uncertainty it creates. If you supplicate, and feed the narcissist's ego, then they will be able to relax, relatively certain that you won't step out of line, criticize them, and force them to confront the fragile nature of their false-self.

But if you are arrogant, it is like a priming stimulus. Suddenly their world is not under control, and it will affect how they respond to all future stimuli. Inside, the paranoia produced by their innate insecurity tells them that an attack may be coming, they brace for it, and then eventually, because you are so arrogant, it hits. They endure both the fear of the attack, the discomfort of bracing for it, and the agony of it. Just as the bullet you don't see coming will often pass through your flesh painlessly, the amygdala hijack you do see coming combines the pain of anticipation with the frustration of bracing, only to culminate in an agony that you have been well-prepared to experience very intensely.

Then, just as the pain of the hijack subsides, the arrogance of their opponent forces the narcissist to brace immediately, because they know another attack is coming, sooner or later. Combined with a mixture of other hijacking stimuli, the constancy of stimulation produced by an arrogant countenance is enormously exhausting to the narcissist, and highly unpleasant.

I have found that if a narcissist does exhibit arrogance, in part to irritate the amygdalae of others, then some subtleties in how that narcissist exhibits his arrogance may be attempts by him to make his countenance maximally irritating - based upon his understanding of what he would find most irritating himself. When this is the case, he is offering a goldmine of intelligence on what would irritate him most effectively. For this reason, I would examine such a narcissist closely, see how he exhibits his arrogance, and then mirror his style of arrogance back at him. Is it intellectual, as if everyone else is an idiot? Is it moral, as if only he is truly good? Is it positional, as if he is a natural leader, and everyone else is a mere serf? Is it appearance based? Always remember, the narcissist is a mirror, reflecting back the types of behaviors which would most irritate them.

Out-grouping

When interacting socially, narcissists are snakes in the grass. One of their major objectives when dealing with those they dislike is to alienate their targets from any social group to which they belong. They do this because they themselves require social validation to support the false reality that they construct to shield their amygdala from stimulation. As long as the group accepts the narcissist and their false reality, the narcissist can cling to the belief that they are somehow normal, or even superior. It is this social validation which serves as a crucial psychological crutch, shielding them from the pain that would result from an honest self-assessment of what they are. Projecting this psychology on others, the narcissist will assume that group-affiliation is just as vitally important to you. As a result, they will seek to disrupt your group affiliations as a way to both, try to disrupt the group-validation of the false reality they assume you have, and preserve this vital psychological crutch for themselves.

Sometimes, your presence can somehow become amygdala stimulating to the narcissist. Perhaps you have taken to purposefully amygdala hijacking them. Perhaps you have begun to realize what the narcissist is, and this risk of exposure is beginning to elicit panic in the narcissist. Perhaps the narcissist is merely afraid that you will try to get them ejected from the group. Or perhaps you are merely so successful and happy that the narcissist can't stand the sight of you (since you remind them of their own failure and misery), despite your being wholly oblivious to the presence of any animosity whatsoever. In such cases, the narcissist will seek to see you ejected from the group, in an effort to remove your amygdala-stimulating quality from their immediate proximity. Again, this occurs as a mechanical means by which the narcissist is attempting to hack their own amygdala, to shut it off. You remind them that they are pathetic, so you need to be removed from their immediate vicinity so they won't see you, and their brain can shut off their amygdala. They also need you identified as "bad" within the group, so they can tell themselves that as your enemy, they are "good." This may happen so primally, that they themselves don't even realize this is the mechanism driving them. They jump right to assuming you are evil, and they are doing good by attacking you.

Since normal people are not dependent on group-validation, and their lives are not spent spinning dense webs of Machiavellian deceptions to control their social networks, normal people will not actively focus on maintaining their own group affiliation, or on disrupting the group affiliation of others. If they like their group, they will tend to passively assume that their own positive emotions for the group, and their own normal behavior will just naturally result in affiliation with the group. Similarly, they will not seek to actively degrade the affiliation of another with the group, assuming that the psychology of the other will either fit into the group, or not, and their respective affiliation will sort itself out. Not so with the narcissist.

This psychological quality of the narcissist is the foundation of what will be referred to here as the out-grouping attack. I found this to be an extraordinarily potent attack when wielded properly. We will cover it mainly because an understanding of it is probably vital to an understanding of how the narcissist relates to the social milieu.

Out-grouping means making an argument to a narcissist, which if made in front of others, is designed to alienate the narcissist from the group. Until now, you've probably argued based upon concepts of right or wrong, logical or illogical, or good or bad. These are all reality-based concepts, and as a result, of little meaning to the narcissist. Out-grouping is designed to show, not what is right or wrong, but how the narcissist espouses things which the group doesn't like.

As an example, examine the arguments over gun-control. There is much evidence that gun-control actually increases crime. John Lott's book *More Guns Less Crime*[1] showed pretty conclusively that when you restrict lawful citizens from carrying guns it emboldens criminals to attack the now unarmed population, and confrontational/violent crime rises statistically. Conversely when you loosen gun laws, and law-abiding citizens begin to bear arms, they become a threat to criminals, and confrontational/violent crime diminishes. Sure enough, after more than a decade spent loosening the regulations hampering law-abiding citizens from owning and carrying guns, we see lower crime rates everywhere it has been done. The criminals don't want to do violent crime if they may get shot by their victims, and the law-abiding citizens owning and carrying guns have turned out to be quite responsible with them, according to the statistics.

Gun-control advocates have no logical argument to support gun-control among the law-abiding based on lowering crime statistics, so what do they argue? Guns kill kids, and by extension, if you oppose gun control, you support killing kids. That is an out-grouping argument. It is an attempt to out-group the pro-gun movement, not by showing them to be logically incorrect in their assertions, or even by showing factually how the pro-gun movement is espousing something tangibly bad, but rather by trying to make the pro-gun position noxious emotionally to the observing audience, so the observing audience will turn on them. Notice how this is not an argument to be won factually. It is strictly an emotional power play, directed at the opponent's group affiliation.

The panic produced by the out-grouping attack is triggered by the narcissist's amygdala sensing the potential for being socially rejected by others. In studies of brain activity, one of the most potent ACC-activating stimuli is the pain of social exclusion. If the narcissist has nobody to help them assert their false reality, where they are normal, and their enemies are wrong, the narcissist is much less able to deny their

---

[1]   Lott, J. (1998). More Guns Less Crime. Chicago, IL: University of Chicago Press.

own nature to themselves. There may be some additional quality to social exclusion, relating to childhood experiences conditioning a real panic response to it in the narcissist.

I have found that out-grouping attacks are best delivered in front of a group. They consist of dropping facts, ideas, or anecdotes which will portray your target as somehow incompatible with the group, or pointing out some emotional facet of their argument which is noxious to the group.

Are your friends Republicans? I would point out jokingly that the narcissist voted for Carter, and then congratulate him on his principles while rolling your eyes and laughing. Nobody will notice anything amiss if your humorous vibe is right, but your narcissist's amygdala will go into high gear – it is how they are designed. I would innocently ask about some incident from their past which would highlight a negative fact the group would find disquieting. If the narcissist makes an assertion, find a counterargument, or example of their idea implemented, which makes the narcissist's assertion somehow noxious to the morality of the group. Steer the topic of conversation to some trait the narcissist has exhibited, which the group would reject or despise. Call them out publicly on bad behavior, or dishonesty, and do so as if you are speaking for the group.

The narcissist's ideal amygdala-assuaging outcome would be the adoration of the group. Your goal is to present to your narcissist some stimulus indicating that the group will despise them, and eject them from its membership.

To us, such an act would be seen as gauche and petty. But to the narcissist, out-grouping is a white hot bolt of lightening, right through their amygdala. They need that group validation to support their false reality, so they can function mentally, and you are stripping it from them, by force. Again, if you are normal, you will not be able to understand much of this. You will have to try it, and press these buttons in the narcissist's head, until you push their brain past the point of neurological failure.

For those wondering, handling a narcissist who is trying to out-group you will be covered in a later chapter.

Forcing to Choose and Preventing Machiavellianism

One thing narcissists want to do is play both sides. You will see it in politics, where Liberals want to be recognized as Americans, but also support terrorists, immigrants, and other outsiders against their own countrymen (so they can't be blamed by anyone, or out-grouped anywhere). Or they want police protection, yet they will also curry favor with criminals, supporting lax sentencing and strict restrictions on the police department's use of force against criminals. You will also see it in non-political interactions, where the narcissist will try to have their cake and eat it too, such as by acting as your friend, and yet portraying some violation of loyalty to you as something they didn't want to do, but had to do, due to circumstances.

If you want to see a narcissist in total ecstasy, and fully relieve all of the stress on their amygdala, simply let them screw you over completely, tell them it wasn't their fault because they had no choice, and then pledge your undying love and loyalty to them. Given that scenario, a narcissist would actually adopt that as truth themselves, telling themselves that they are really a good, loyal person. At the same time, they would feel immensely fortunate and delighted to have been gifted with circumstances that allowed them to act out against you without any consequence.

If you wish to pile stress on their amygdala, make it so their transgressions have cost, and they are unable to act out against you, in any way, without direct consequence. Call them out openly on bad behavior, so they have to endure consequence. Create circumstances where they have to make the painful choice of not injuring you and your interests, or destroying their relationship with you and being outed publicly as a self-absorbed, evil person, who derives pleasure from the misfortunes of those around them.

If you are dealing with a political narcissist, call them out on their attempt to play both sides. Either you are with your fellow American citizens, or you are with the foreign immigrants. Either you are with the police, or you are with the criminals. Either you are with the bureaucrats or you are with the citizens. Either you want America to win, or you support outsiders against us. As one Marine once put it in a debate with Mike Wallace, tell them that, *"you can't have it both ways."*[1]

As we have maintained, narcissists are highly averse to any negative cognitive stimulus. They want to find a way to avoid all the bad. Playing both sides and having their cake and eating it too - these are tools which the narcissist wields purposefully, if unconsciously, to try and minimize negative stimuli within their brain. By pursuing this path, they can avoid all negative stimuli, even when they ostensibly should have to pick one, if you allow them to.

View their behavior as a mechanical hack of their brain circuitry, recognize its purpose, and then recognize that they are willing to delude themselves to avoid the pain of choosing. If I were to use this as a hijack, I would manipulate their perceptions so that they have to pick a poison, emphasize to them that they must chose one, and then emphasize the negative consequences of both options. If need be, use the threat of out-grouping to force a choice ("George Bush's *with us or against us"* line on terrorism, and it's amygdala-stimulating effect on liberals comes to mind).

The Bad Two-fer

This is a cognitive hack of the narcissist's brain circuitry that is almost the direct inverse of the hack that the narcissist attempts to use to shield themselves, when playing both sides, or having their cake and eating it too. Here, you will present a perception of circumstances to the narcissist that is designed to force them to chose between two bad perceptions of themselves, or their circumstances. Usually, the beginning of such a hijack will lay a logical case for each option, and the ending of such a hijack will sound something like, *"...either you are ignorant, or immoral!"*

---

[1]   From the Touching the Raw Amygdala series on debating leftists with amygdala hijacks. Marine Colonel George M. Connell left Mike Wallace savaged with an epic amygdala hijack, which included a diminution of stature attack, an out-grouping attack, and a forcing to choose attack, all combined with mechanical hijacks as well. Wallace was left a depressed, dejected mess, unable to even make eye contact. The entire series, including a link to the video, can be found here : http://www.anonymousconservative.com/blog/touching-the-raw-amygdala-an-analysis-of-liberal-debate-tactics-preface/

In my experience, this is an incredibly powerful technique, and amenable to application with all manner of harshness or subtlety. I have used this openly and ruthlessly, as above, in a full blown argument to drive the narcissist mad, and I have used this covertly, by offering the bad choices more gently, and more reticently.

One interesting thing about the narcissist brain is the cognitive degradation which occurs when they feel stalked by the panic of a negative stimulus. They literally cannot think clearly. Again, we encounter negativity all of the time. It is there, but unless it involves our immediate and utter ruination or dismemberment, we usually assign it a relatively low priority, and take note of it. However it doesn't dominate us. Not so the narcissist – this fundamental cognitive difference is why they are so bizarre. Every move, every action is a conditioned behavior designed specifically to shield their amygdala from any negativity.

Here, when I would present two bad stimuli to the narcissist, and direct them to choose one, their amygdala will flag the first one cursorily as bad, initiate immediate denial, blockage, and panic, switch to focus on the other option, flag it cursorily as bad, initiate immediate denial, blockage, and panic responses, and return to the first option, repeating the procedure.

In a normal brain, only mildly sensitive to negativity, an examination of both options simultaneously will then occur, followed by a weighing of each option's negativity relative to the other. This would usually be followed by a wide-ranging scan for other potential options that might not have been considered, which might prove less negative than the two proffered options. If a calm assessment of reality indicates that you will need to embrace one of the bad options, you will try to embrace the less bad option, and then try to adapt your behavior to mitigate, as much as possible, the negativity you will endure.

In the most afflicted narcissist, my experience indicates that none of this will happen. They will be so overwhelmed by the negative stimuli which flood over them, as they cursorily peek at each option through slit thin, half covered, neurological eyes, that they will just jump back and forth, from a peek at one option and a shock, to a peek at the other followed by a shock, and then back to the first, only to be shocked again. If you present the two options properly, and refocus the narcissist on each a few times, you can watch as they sink into a spiral of depression and horror, and lose the ability to think rationally. It is tremendously exhausting to their amygdala.

The bad two-fer you offer can be an examination of the situation the narcissist is in. Sometimes I would postulate to my narcissist, either you do this and you are screwed, or you do this and you are screwed. I would follow it up with a vocalization of my astonishment at how he was really trapped in a horrible spot, and would have to endure something really bad, and how awful it was. I'd rehash the situation a few times, marveling at it's scope, sympathizing with his plight, amazed at how inescapable it was.

I have also found the bad twofer useful when analyzing motives of a narcissist. Either things are this way, and you are evil, or things are this way, and you are the most inept person I have ever met. (As will be explained later, the use of inept, rather than stupid, is purposeful.)

In my experience, the bad twofer is also effective in debates with a narcissist. There you would couch the opponent's argument as either stature-diminishing, ignorant, immoral, or unconcerned with the welfare of the group (out-grouping). Or one could structure events so the narcissist would be either forced at some point to embrace failure in one regard, or another. Of course, the most powerful form would be any bad two-fer which injured the narcissist's false-self, such as, 'either you are a born loser with the worst luck imaginable, or you are a totally incompetent failure.'

You get the idea of how it works. What a bad-twofer is doing is inserting a computer program in the narcissist's brain that presents two negative stimuli to their consciousness, combined with a direction to actively select either one or the other, and limiting the selection to one of those two choices. Given the command in their operating system to not look too closely, or think too much, about anything bad, and to not select a bad option, the effect can be quite powerful. Although in my experience, one bad-twofer did not a melt-down make, I found I could usually get a good, blank, glossy-eyed stare, which is the hallmark of an amygdala that was just jolted substantially. The full meltdown is not far off at that point.

Ridicule

Ridicule is such an amazingly powerful weapon in attacking the narcissist, it deserves its own section. I am unclear specifically why it is so powerful. Some research shows that narcissists prefer seeing sad faces, so perhaps the amusement in faces as people ridicule the narcissist adds to their agony. Or perhaps when you reach the point that people are not only saying you are bad, they are laughing about how bad you are, you are beyond hope of reversing their opinions, and this hopeless level of out-grouping conveys a feeling of powerlessness that further shocks the narcissist. Or perhaps if people are laughing at you, then they have no respect for you, and you have lost all possibility of attaining any sort of high social standing. If that were the case, a narcissist would innately perceive that they would never be able to construct an amygdala-shielding false reality supported by their peers again. It could be a combination of all of those things, I don't know.

What I do know is that there are few weapons as powerful in social situations as making a comment that provokes laughter at the narcissist's foibles, and then elbowing others as you point at the narcissist, to get the observers laughing at the narcissist too. If it is combined with a bad two-fer, creating a joke with two choices about how bad the narcissist has it, or what a loser they are, and then everyone begins laughing at it, the narcissist will be in agony.

Make Diminutives Relate to Reality

Narcissists need to tell themselves that they are superior, to prevent themselves from performing an honest assessment of their own inferiority. Given this, it is tempting to assume that pointing out some negative trait, such as their stupidity, and labeling it such, will function to burst the bubble of their false reality, and provoke some amygdala stimulation.

Increasingly however, I have found that labeling the narcissist "*stupid*" may not have as potent an amygdala-simulating effect as one would desire. I have known narcissists who have seemingly embraced being labeled as stupid by close relatives, recognizing that such a label will shield them from any consequences for their covertly hostile actions. I can think of one who acts Gary-Busey-bizarre, and embraces their oddball/mentally-retarded reputation, because that reputation gives them free reign to attack other's amygdalae without consequence.

After a lifetime of acting out against people, and getting away with it due to being viewed as dull, many narcissists seem to view being seen by peers as stupid as a mark of power, from the perspective of their craft. Some will even seem amused at being called stupid, apparently viewing it as a sign of their success at deceiving their targets in a way which will allow them to act as they please, and get away with anything.

Furthermore, the label will be viewed as wholly unrelated to reality by the narcissist, and thus not shock their amygdala, since they know that the people labeling them stupid are about to be subjected to all manner of purposeful abuse, without even being aware of it. Given how much slack most normal people afford the narcissist in their lives, due to attributing their behavior to stupidity rather than malice, who can blame the narcissist for viewing their victims as the ones who were really stupid, and thereby feeling superior themselves by comparison?

Instead of stupid, I use words which relate directly to a provable reality, rather than such a subjective assessment. This prevents the narcissist from neutralizing the argument in their mind with some caveat relating to vagueness or subjectivity (as they have been conditioned to do from childhood).

Incompetence or ineptness is something more concrete and provable, if it is based on a cold, hard performance metric which shows that they failed at something tangible (obviously the metric should be used immediately to substantiate the hijack, and tie it to an inarguable reality). Stupid is more subjective, and prone to vagaries of interpretation, or even deceit. One can argue stupidity, but one cannot argue if one was fired. One can argue the ugliness of someone's personality, one cannot argue if no member of their family will talk to them. One can argue the word loser, one cannot argue the physical manifestations in one's life, such as total lack of friends, low income, etc. One can argue likability, but one cannot argue a demonstrable lie to the group.

If you attack the narcissist's amygdala with an attack which offers the narcissist the ability, in any way, to shield their amygdala with some argument invalidating your assertion, based on vagueness or subjectivity, that amygdala hijack will often fail. For that reason, I always try to pierce their bubble of false reality with a sword of truth and reality, rather than any assertions which could prove subjective. I always focus their amygdala on a metric of failure which undeniably shows that the only means of honestly judging them has been performed, and they have been judged a failure objectively – and will be so judged by anyone else who examines that situation.

I Know That You Know

The worst narcissists can be horribly frustrating to interact with, in large part because they will, like a spy, sink into a deep-cover identity, designed to shield them from any consequences for their actions. This deep cover will have, as its final layer, a personality that is so detached from reality that they will seemingly be unaware of their own lies and malfeasance. But there will be some awareness of their true nature, vague as it may be.

Explain to them, (as if a confidant), that someone else will know they are lying, and they will tell you, *"He can't tell if I'm lying. He has no idea what I'm thinking. I could easily believe that to be true myself. He's not in my head. He doesn't know my thoughts."* Because of that, they will convince themselves that since it can't be proven to be a lie, it could be true, and if it could be true, it isn't lying – and since it isn't lying, it therefore must be true, even though they themselves know it is not. I saw this with my own favorite narcissist.

Later, as our relationship soured, he would insist on the most egregious falsehoods to me, and refuse to acknowledge any ability to see the falsehood himself. He seemed to truly believe that if I couldn't prove that he knew it was false, then it wasn't a lie. His final amygdala shield was an assertion he made to his own brain, that I had no idea what he was thinking, and could never prove that he knew he was lying.

It would sometimes prevent a full hijacking of his amygdala, and was most frustrating. Finally, I found a way to short circuit this defense. I would engage him with questions, until I could find some small inconsistency in his assertions – a place where he altered his initial assertion, to fill in a gap in his logic. Once I found any minor change in his story, I would point out his original story, point out the changed story, and then say, *"You just changed the story you were telling me.*

That tells me, YOU KNOW that what you are saying is untrue. And now, I KNOW, THAT YOU KNOW, exactly what you are, and exactly what you are doing."

I only needed to do this once, and it set up a simple way to punish my favorite narcissist whenever he would try to argue with me like that in the future.

My first step was to find one case where rigorous cross examination made him change his story, to keep from looking like a liar. This is not that hard. Narcissists often bolster their false reality's structural strength in their own mind by over-emphasizing their case. Rather than say he didn't lie once, a narcissist will assert he never lies, and never would lie. I would call up one small lie he told once, and then use the line above when he adjusts his statement. Maybe he claims that he never deviates from a schedule so he couldn't have done something. I would emphasize to him the aspect of that statement that is false. I would point out that one day years back when he missed that schedule for some reason. He'd then say, *"Well, I missed it that day, yeah, but..."* I would then cut in and say, *"You're changing your story, which tells me that you know it's untrue. You're adjusting it as you go along. You Know!* (look shocked) *And now I know, that you know, that is untrue!"*

I'd emphasize the *"I know, you know"* part of that statement, because I would be burning it into his amygdala, as a concrete reminder that I know that he knows. In the future, I'd want that short statement in his head, like a switch ready to be tripped, to force him to realize that I know he knows. Whenever I used it, it was like violating his last safe space, and taking away the last defense to the amygdala hijack in his arsenal.

Again, the narcissist is not a clear thinker, especially in the midst of confrontation. I wouldn't need to assemble a clear logical argument showing that his entire statement was provably false. The narcissist is looking at vague themes, rather than a highly relevance-weighed, detailed examination of the facts and their relation to his initial claim. So I'd need one small detail where he was forced to back down and change his initial assertion, so within his head a vague image of having been caught-out emerged. Once I'd created that vague perception of having failed to deceive me, and having been caught red-handed trying, I'd focus the narcissist on it. His defective amygdala would blow it out of proportion for me, and convey to his brain the concept that he had been caught, that I knew, that I knew he knew I knew, and that all was now lost.

Once I found the opportunity to deliver the above line, all future interactions with my main narcissist became much easier. From that moment forward, whenever he would assert things I knew were false, and I wanted to snap him back to reality, I delivered the line, *"I know that you know exactly what you are, and exactly what you are doing – I know... that YOU know...."*

Piercing that last bubble of false reality, where the narcissist denies their own intent or awareness, based upon the fact that you couldn't unravel what is going on in their head, is like penetrating the last safe space in their head, and inserting a few lines of programing code to make invading it even easier in the future. By the time my favorite narcissist and I parted ways, I could elicit an expression of utter dejection on his face merely by dismissing his phoney assertions of false realities with a disgusted, rejecting facial expression as I shook my head disappointedly, locked burning eye contact, and delivered the simple, emphasized statement that, *"I know, that YOU know."*

Gaslighting

There are two different definitions you will see attributed to the term gaslighting. One describes its most extreme form, consisting of a narcissist gradually breaking down a victim, and then attributing the victim's breakdown to a mental illness - a diagnosis which unaware victims, mentally disoriented by their bizarre interactions with such a defective psychology, will often concur with and submit to. In some cases, the narcissist has even gone so far as to have the victim committed to institutional care, and the victim, suffering mentally and unable to see the narcissist's role in their suffering, has acquiesced to the care in the hopes of being cured of their mental inability to function in their (narcissist filled) environment. During all of this the narcissist plays the role of selfless and loyal partner, only seeking what is best for their victim, ofttimes as they take control of bank accounts, sell homes, and reorganize their life in the manner they wanted, all along.

What the narcissist gets from such actions is the relief of seeing someone who is worse off than they are, the external validation of their mental state as being stable relative to that of their victims, and the ability to portray themselves both to outsiders (and to their own mind), as selfless, sacrificing, mentally sane, and loyal.

The other definition of gaslighting is a broader definition, encompassing any alteration of an individual's perception of reality through deception. One friend told me the story of a female relative of his. Her husband took a sleeping medication. Occasionally he would come home late, inebriated from a night of heavy drinking, take his sleeping medication, and go to bed. The next morning he would wake up with strange, clearly defined bruises all over his face. He would wonder to his wife what had happened, and she would say he must have been really drunk if he couldn't remember how he got them.

It turned out that the truth was that she, irritated by his wanton drinking and carousing, had wanted him to drink less. So she decided to make drinking heavily seem to precipitate negative consequences that he would then seek to avoid by curtailing his alcohol consumption. Basically she waited until his drunkenness and sleep medication had combined their effects. She would then take a stiletto high heel, and use it like a hammer all over his face, lightly at first, so as to determine his level of unconsciousness, but increasing in force until it could produce the requisite pattern of unique bruising. Her husband never found out, but continued his drinking, and eventually they divorced for other reasons. Recently her new husband was heard commenting on how his sleep medication had him sleep walking. He knew only because he would wake up with all sorts of strange bruises all over his body, but no memory of how he had gotten them. He was certain that he was walking into things while asleep, putting himself back to bed, and the bruises that he saw when he woke up were the evidence.

Gaslighting can consist of taking all of a husband's pants in for tailoring to a smaller size, so when he tries to put them on in the future he feels as if he has gotten fatter. One book recommended buying hats of different sizes that match your target's, giving them all the same distinctive markings of use, and then swapping them periodically, so he will think his head is swelling and shrinking for unknown reasons. More ominously, it can consist of mild poisoning, to initiate the symptoms of disease, or just constant denigration to make a person think they are less worthy than they are, in reality.

As with most narcissist attacks, gaslighting is probably more effective on the narcissist than it is on normal people. Narcissists have conditioned themselves to not look too closely at the world, lest the world appear unpleasant at first glance. When reality terrifies you to the point that you willingly ignore it, despite a constant stream of negative consequences, you end up particularly vulnerable to seeing your perceptions of reality altered.

Adding to the mix is a defective amygdala that can't focus properly on facts or logic. Instead, their amygdalae are apparently substituting vague summaries and cursory examinations of only the broadest stimuli presented to it, in an effort to avoid being caught staring intently at some concept or idea that happens across their radar and elicits pain or negativity. Even as this causes all of the horrible symptoms of narcissism, it also makes it easier for you to guide their amygdala's focus to the irrelevant, emphasize the relevance of the unimportant, overwhelm with feelings and emotions not called for by reality, and couch evidence of one thing as actually supportive of another. (Only such a psychology would try to assert that massive blizzards are, in actuality, further evidence of anthropogenic global warming.) In my experience, the narcissist will often be so overwhelmed by the negative emotional response to bad news, that they will not closely examine the factual and logical reasoning leading up to the bad news to begin with.

It is also worth noting that narcissists seem unusually dependent on the opinions of the group. Perhaps they are aware that they cannot trust their own emotion-riddled perceptions, or that they cannot examine reality close enough to hold a truly trustworthy opinion of reality, and thus any belief of the group will, by necessity, carry the weight of reality with them. When your reality is defined by the group, your reality is really defined by the individual who molds the reality that the group adopts. It is due to this self-realization that the Narcissist places undue emphasis on being the central information hub, and seeks to drive any individual who opposes their control of the information flow away from the group, through any means necessary, moral or immoral.

Using the Third Person

Psychiatrist Milton Erickson found that if he told his patients things about themselves which they didn't want to hear, they would often dismiss him out of hand, and consciously block out the information through aggressive denial. That would have been their amygdala encountering negativity, and choosing to de-emphasize the importance of the data, regardless of logic, rather than face it.

Dr. Erickson got around this by telling the patients stories about other people, with similar problems. He would detail what was wrong with these other people, and how they would fix their own problem. Once the criticisms weren't seen by his patients as personal attacks, or even relating to them personally, they became more open to thinking about the criticism, and the potential solutions. I have both seen this used by others, and used it myself to get a piece of information into a narcissist's head, and past the defensive denial mechanism in their brain.

As an example, if you lay a hijacking stimulus on a narcissist, such as the concept that they are not liked by others, they will often scoff, and reject any possibility of their dislike-ability. Once the denial has begun, getting supporting facts into their head, or even getting them to ponder the possibility of the stimulus itself can be unusually difficult.

However, if you tell a story about someone similar to the narcissist, explain how they do similar things, explain how it is only logical that they should then be unliked because of this, and then lay out how this person is exactly the same as the narcissist, the narcissist will have already followed your logic and reasoning by the time you link him to the unliked individual. Indeed, the desire to castigate others as inferior may have him nodding his head in total agreement with what a defective this other person is, right up until you undeniably link him with them, with a single piece of irrefutable logic. In my experience, this produces a much more powerful hijack, a much more satisfying result, and a much reduced ability on the part of the narcissist to throw up a barrier of denial to the offending concept.

Priming/Bracing

There is a saying that, *"pain perceived is pain achieved."* It means that if someone is made afraid by the threat of pain, it can be just as beneficial to your purposes as actually hurting them. In the case of amygdala hijacks, I have found that a pending hijack perceived, can make the subsequent hijack even more effective. I call this priming/bracing. The effect of priming/bracing is similar to how some people get shot through flesh, and never notice the bullet wound. Not expecting the shot, it passes through them before their brain can register the sensations it produces. By the time they notice they have been shot, the pain is over and gone.

The opposite is knowing that a painful event is coming, imagining it, bracing for it, dreading it, and then watching as it begins, and then focusing specifically on how it slowly fulfills all of your worst imaginations of it.

One of the main functions of the amygdala is that it decides what you will focus upon. The text you are reading right now, is the focus of your attention because your amygdala has flagged it as the most important data to your purposes at the moment. Let a man with a gun suddenly break down your door, and your amygdala will shift your focus away from this text, without you even asking it to. In a moment, this text will be the farthest thing from your mind, and you won't have to do anything to make it so.

In the case of amygdala hijacks, if your target knows you are prone to hijack them, and you do it often enough, they will begin to brace around you, as their amygdala takes their focus and directs it to trying to perceive the coming hijack. Chances are, if you have been around a bad enough narcissist for long enough, you brace around him or her, and this bracing will make their minor and petty irritations have outsized effects on you.

I knew one narcissist who preceded hijacks with a long, drawn out, irritating, whiny, nasal, "Aaahhhh......." vocalization, as if to focus attention fully on himself. (One of his relatives once commented on how they hated that sound - in retrospect, it was priming her.) However, I have seen this most effectively employed by narcissists who use physical hijacks (to be discussed later) to seemingly trigger bracing, before launching their hijacks. The physical hijackers use physical hijacks to set the stage for more complex conceptual hijacks, priming their target's amygdalae to respond maximally to subsequent hijacks. Basically my experience here is that if you can get your narcissist to the point that they are reflexively bracing for some form of amygdala stimulation around you (even if just by constantly hijacking them at every opportunity), a subsequent hijack will have much greater effect. As it begins, they will focus on it more, because they knew it was coming. They will have primed themselves to panic/rage, even entering a mildly panicked/rage-filled state to begin with, and when the real panic/rage finally begins, it will be more pronounced. I have found that all of that adds to the cumulative effect of the hijack, and shortens the time leading to a complete meltdown.

Customizing the Conceptual Amygdala Hijack

Here we will discuss how to customize the amygdala hijacks you would use on your own narcissist. I advise against amygdala hijacking your narcissist, however knowing how to customize amygdala hijacks on your narcissist is still an important skill, as it will help you to better understand where your narcissist came from, and what stimuli are triggering him, and precipitating his rages.

Customizing hijacks involves deeply analyzing what your own narcissist says and how he responds to the world around him, as well as pumping any relatives who grew up with him or her, for information on their childhood. Many narcissists will be found to have unique quirks, and specific fears, most of which will have been created by the unique traumas (often in childhood) that led to their conditions. Ofttimes, the narcissist, lost in the ecstasy of being the center of attention, will foolishly let slip some incident from their past which was so foundational that it will highlight a vital Achilles heel, and give you a profound insight into their psychology. Here, their incessant need to fill the dead air with every thought of their own, and their desire to manipulate you into concessions through eliciting sympathy can be their worst enemies. Listen to the wrongs that they have endured at the hands of an unfair world closely, for those were the amygdala-triggering events which trained them to deny the reality that they can now no longer face.

There can't be a simple guide to tell you exactly what specific themes and concepts will best trigger your narcissist's amygdala, but

83

with careful observation, you can divine these subtle nuances yourself, and learn much about your narcissist in the process. Listen when your narcissist talks about their past, especially their childhood. Do they recount instances which enraged them? What circumstances bothered them most often? Who do they talk about angrily? Is there an event that they appear to actually relive, as they recount it? Narcissists love to talk about themselves, and explain the hardships they endured at length, to try and manipulate out of you, the social currency of sympathy. Use that intelligence to begin figuring out what triggered their amygdala when they were young, and conditioned it to fire off. That will usually give you an idea of what similar circumstances and themes will trigger their amygdala when they are older. However, bear in mind that the most traumatic event which created the disorder will probably only be spoken of tangentially, in small pieces, which will need to be woven together. Bob spoke of the back-brace, spoke of the teasing, spoke of the optical migraine, and spoke of the throwing up, but it took investigation among his relatives to piece them all together into one event.

It helps when performing the analysis of how this data relates to the present, to understand that the narcissist will generally not assign each individual in their life a unique role, and be fully aware of that individual's unique nature within their life. I have found that, perhaps due to viewing the world vaguely, narcissists will tend to shoehorn people they know as adults into a small set of intellectual cubbyholes that they also use to store personalities from their childhood. Thus a wife may actually occupy a position in his mind that originally was home to his mother's visage. Because of this, he may attribute characteristics of his mother to his wife, blame his wife for transgressions his mother committed when he was a child, view her behaviors in the frame of mind that he viewed his mother's, and even occasionally, absentmindedly refer to her as his mother, or by his mother's name. Often younger people will occupy the cubbyholes of younger siblings, bosses will occupy the cubbyholes of fathers, and potential threats (or just manly men) will end up in the cubbyholes of older siblings or childhood bullies.

This is useful, since if your narcissist was conditioned to rage in childhood by a younger brother who got great gifts from their mother (which he became conditioned to subsequently break "accidentally" to relieve the amygdala stress), and in adulthood a younger male wins the lottery, that adult visage will likely trigger many similar emotions and behavioral urges to the childhood one. That modern event will offer critical insight into how your narcissistic robot was programmed in childhood. You will see this in politics, where many tyrannical leaders will often come from dysfunctional and unpleasant childhoods, spent constantly angry that they weren't in full control of everyone and everything in their environment. As adults, such individuals can usually be hijacked easily by presenting to them images of real cases of their own impotence as adults. If you emphasize to them their own impotence, patheity, and frustration, you can watch as the pressure builds.

Another method of unraveling your narcissist is to ask, what does the narcissist use to attack you, to trigger your amygdala? Often the narcissist will plan their attack on you by imagining what would bother them the most. Does your narcissist criticize your appearance? If so, then they are likely insecure about their own appearance. Do they try to demean your accomplishments? That is what would bother them. Do they try to bully you? They likely would be traumatized by feeling the impotence of being bullied themselves.

Again, my impression is that the narcissist's habit of blinding themselves to the world around them, to dull the pain it causes, eventually affects every aspect of their perception of the world around them. It leaves them less able to examine the world around them, and less able to ruminate on it. Thus, instead of examining you honestly, and looking for your weaknesses, the narcissist will, without thought, simply imagine that you are the same as he is, and then try to formulate a means of attack based on that. Thus many attacks become what would most traumatize them.

Finally, many of us have seen the narcissistic rage. You, while having an innocent conversation, say something innocuous, and suddenly your narcissist is a raging mess. As you were talking, some idea or theme you presented was read by the narcissist, and made him think about something painful. Reflexively, he burst into a rage, and freaked out, until you retreated. Whatever that idea was, it was a reality he needed to deny, and its contemplation triggered his amygdala powerfully.

As tough as it is, pay close attention when interacting with your narcissist. When you provoke a rage, remember what preceded it. Whatever it was, will be prime amygdala triggering material. There is nothing more powerful to trigger an amygdala hijack than the reality the narcissist denies. Identify that reality, and understand how your presentation of it to the narcissist was so painful, and you will have a critical insight into their mind.

Some narcissists will freak out when presented with a theme of inferiority relative to peers, due to an insecurity and perception of competition with equals that was generated through years of sibling rivalries, or months spent hanging by their underwear from the gym lockers at school. Others will have spent their entire youth repetitively blaming a relative, such as their mother, for every hardship that they suffered, and they will subsequently freak out at the theme of a woman interfering with their plans, foisting hardship upon them in some way, or just enjoying their lives happily. Others may be conditioned to freak out when frustrated in some effort, due to a childhood spent being frustrated by a passive aggressive sibling, which developed all the neural pathways to produce that response reflexively. Others may have been conditioned by parental abandonment, or parental disregard of their worth, or the refusal of a parent to support them over a step-parent when morally wronged by said step-parent. Still others will be triggered by the visage of those who have something that they don't, due to a childhood spent watching other children acquire and enjoy things that they themselves could never dream of.

Learn everything you possibly can. You never know when a small, seemingly insignificant piece of information, can end up combining with some later insight, and prove critical to a fuller understanding later on.

Chapter Eleven

*Physical/Mechanical Amygdala Hijacks*____

If you are going to understand your interactions with a narcissist, it is important to understand the full panoply of amygdala triggering stimuli, and how they trigger aversive stimulus, thus motivating behaviors and affecting cognition. The difference between a conceptual amygdala hijack and a physical/mechanical amygdala hijack is that where the conceptual hijack requires presentation of a complex idea that must be ruminated upon to precipitate the hijack, the physical/mechanical hijack relies on a physical, reflexive response to a non-conceptual stimulus that is more primal in nature. To picture a physical/mechanical amygdala hijack, try this visualization experiment. Visualize the discomfort produced by a creepy individual you meet at a party, invading your physical space by getting uncomfortably close to you, placing their hands on you contrary to your wishes (even in a sexual fashion), and making fast motions around your face as they talk about something sexually disgusting. All of those are primal urges and reflexes, which produce amygdala stimulation. That discomfort you will feel is aversive stimulus, and as you are feeling it, your amygdala is becoming more trigger-able, less able to perform rational logic, and more sensitive to triggering stimuli which you would otherwise be able to process cogently. Of course in the narcissist, I am convinced that those sensations are several-fold worse, and the debilitating effects they have on cognition are vastly more powerful.

For this reason, I have found that my amygdala hijacks were more easily engendered when I combined the conceptual hijack with physical mechanical hijacks to amplify their effects.

Eye Contact

Direct, unblinking eye contact is a potent amygdala stimulant. Instinctually, it is a stimulus which is associated with conflict - a situation which requires heightened amygdala activity to discern important information, focus you upon it, and drive behavior.

On several occasions I have noted that heavily hijacked individuals will unconsciously try to rein in their hijacked amygdala's hyperactivity by assiduously avoiding eye contact, often by looking down at the ground, in an exaggerated fashion similar to that displayed by severely afflicted autistic children. My own favorite narcissist, on several occasions, would bark, "*Look at me!*," as he attempted hijacks on individuals who were not making eye contact with him. He would often follow up such a command with a statement about how it was disrespectful, or rude to not look at someone who was talking to you, before continuing his hijack. When I would observe this, I mistook it for an individual who wished to be the center of attention, however I now believe he found eye contact subtly stressful, and thus when he wished to stress others he would insist upon it.

I should note that it is possible that one would get a greater response focusing on one eye over the other, due to one eye's visual inputs into the brain being dominant over the other (eye dominance is actually a well characterized phenomenon). Although I have not experimented with narcissists specifically, I have noted slightly differing times to eye aversion with dogs (a sign of submission triggered by amygdala activation), based on which eye I locked eye contact with. If this is the case, most people would have to determine through experimentation which eye yielded a quicker aversion of eye contact, a faster acceleration of stress, or a shorter time to amygdala meltdown, since eye dominance varies among individuals, and is usually difficult to perceive externally, for most people.

Space Invasion

Research clearly shows that the amygdala is activated by proximity of other individuals, even just the proximity of researchers to the test subject in an fMRI brain scanner. We all have a perception of our own personal space. When this space is invaded we begin to experience subtle discomfort. Although not debilitating, when you combine this discomfort, with other means of amygdala stimulation, and the narcissist's inherently weak amygdala function, my experience has been that it will speed the time to breakdown, and even condition the narcissist's amygdala and ACC to go on high alert in your presence.

Unpredictability/Unfamiliarity

The amygdala will scan the environment, and disregard predictable stimuli. Do you feel your watch on your wrist? You don't because your amygdala has registered it as a familiar stimulus, and disregarded the sensation it produces. Ever listen to a new song, and find yourself totally focused on it? It is unpredictable. Ever zone out during a favorite song, only to find it is suddenly over, and you weren't even listening? It was a predictable audio stimulus, and even though you loved listening to it, your amygdala disregarded it to focus on something else. Ever walk past a crazy homeless man doing crazy things? He was unpredictable, and that was your amygdala turning on and scanning the data stream for any sign of threat, in response to the unpredictability. Remember seeing exactly how the bushes looked outside your house as you left for work? They are predictable.

Unpredictable stimuli can be movement, changes in vocal tone, facial expression, or conversational topics. A jerky-moving, crazy looking guy, who flicks his hand up in front of your face periodically as he talks, whose voice has a strange quality, and who out of the blue, begins apprising you of embarrassing details about his sex life with his wife, will be unpleasant to be around, because his unpredictability is amygdala stimulating. I am actually picturing a specific individual as I write that, and that individual once commented how he enjoys keeping the people around him off-balance emotionally. I firmly believe all of that strange behavior was a purposely thought out strategy, and even if it wasn't, I can vouch for its effectiveness as an amygdala stimulant.

Physical Contact

Unsolicited physical contact can be amygdala stimulating. Politicians such as Barack Obama frequently make a point of resting their hands comfortably on men they encounter, ostensibly as a way to

89

show friendship and familiarity (as well as dominance), but this action also serves as a mild amygdala stimulant. I have seen narcissists use this to put people off, make them uncomfortable, and keep them off balance. Previously I would have found putting my hands on a guy I met so uncomfortable and awkward, that it would have amygdala hijacked me more than my target. However since recognizing that it is merely a technique designed to activate the amygdala, I find it much easier to laugh to myself as I execute this on narcissists I encounter.

Threat

Not everyone can pull this off, but one stimulus which can turn on an amygdala is perception of threat. If you can appear somewhat threatening and dominant, without diminishing your social standing in any way, this will aid to activate your target's amygdala. Eye contact is can be one way in which threat is subtly communicated, but body posture, attitude, movement, and lack of concern for others can all also convey threat. Threat can also be conveyed through past history, such as having a history of amygdala hijacking your narcissist. Physical size can also serve this purpose. Arnold Schwarzenegger often spoke of the "authority of size," and how just by being big, men would instinctually assume subordinate positions to him in the social hierarchy.

I can think of one narcissist I knew who exhibited a very intense, almost angry eye appearance, something which at times was strangely at odds with the manner in which he spoke. I previously would have disregarded such a mien as coincidental, but knowing what I know now, I would not rule out that his intense look, (combined with a vocal tone that was discordant with his appearance) was a practiced technique designed to try and place the amygdala activity of other people under some degree of control.

The Stillface Mien

I still do not know exactly why this is such a powerful technique to freak out narcissists (though a mechanism will be proposed in the next section), but it is. In my opinion, and the experience of many who have written me, it is likely one of the most powerful techniques in this book. Even stranger, I am almost certain that after reading all of the following, you will not believe that it could possibly have nearly the power it does. You will be wrong – and it should only take one or two implementations of it to blow your mind.

Decades ago, a researcher did what was called the Stillface Experiment. It was a horrible experiment, and there are videos of it online for those who wish to view it.[1] Basically in the experiment, a baby was restrained in a seat, and his mother would sit opposite him, facing him. The baby would do what babies do, goo-ing and gaa-ing as he swung his arms around, and the mother would smile and laugh back at him. Up until this point, all was fine and everything was normal.

As the experiment began, the mother would suddenly adopt a totally blank, unchanging facial expression, as if she were a mannequin, and cease responding to the baby's antics. Initially the baby would look confused, and then swing his arms harder, and goo and gaa with even more enthusiasm, to get her attention. Then, after a confused pause, the baby would grow concerned that he wasn't getting any emotional feedback, and he would begin to cry and bounce up and down in his seat, waving his arms in a vain attempt to provoke the mother to do *something*. As the experiment came to an end, the baby would finally begin to experience what appeared to be a seizure, with his back and neck muscles contracting, and bending him backward in a convulsed position, as he screamed uncontrollably, and seemingly lost the ability to physically control his body.

The experiment was designed to show how babies are programmed to want to give an emotional response, and get one back, as well as how not getting the desired response back from its mother will degrade the function of a baby's brain, and create a real cognitive trauma. Today it is often cited as demonstrative of an effect seen in another personality disorder (and perhaps even a means by which that disorder is conditioned) where the afflicted individual acts out desperately in unpredictable manners when dealing with others, solely because they need some sort of emotional response, just as the baby in the Stillface Experiment did.

---

[1]   "Still Face Experiment: Dr. Edward Tronick," (Nov 30, 2009), <https://www.youtube.com/watch?v=apzXGEbZht0>. (Accessed May 1, 2014)

Regardless, I have seen the same effect in many narcissists myself, and heard back from readers that the Stillface mien has worked on many more.

Long before I ever even heard of the Stillface experiment, I was amygdala hijacking my narcissist, still fascinated by this new power I had stumbled upon. He was clearly rapidly losing brain function, and I decided to help things along by feigning immense emotional investment in the hijack, and making elaborate gestures and movements to emphasize every hijack. My thought was that I was overstimulating his brain until he melted down, and the more stimuli I could present to him, including demonstrations of my own emotion, the better.

But my hyper-emotional delivery didn't work, and indeed, it defused the entire hijack, to my great befuddlement. As I displayed the emotions, and became overly dramatic, I watched in puzzlement as my narcissist suddenly seemed to recover. As if by magic, I could see the strength begin to well up within him, and all the panic and depression abate, replaced by smugness, and a sense of authority and control. I made careful note of the change, and the next time, I went the other way, hyper-unemotional, and it was devastating to him.

What was going on? I have no idea. On some level, I suspect the emotional display is probably focusing the narcissist's brain away from the hijacking concepts and themes. The emotional display is distracting the brain with the face-reading functions of the amygdala, among others, and that is somewhat diminishing the effect of the conceptual hijack through distraction.

But I suspect the real issue is something much deeper, rooted in the developmental mechanism underlying the effects seen in the Stillface experiment. Perhaps the narcissist's brain exhibits a stalled development, similar in some way to the baby's, and the lack of emotion in people they deal with simply trips a freak-out circuit in their brain. Perhaps this need for emotional response motivates some of their emotion-manipulating behaviors. Whatever the mechanism, the Stillface Mien is a potent amygdala stimulant to hijack a narcissist.

Since I have begun doing it, I have found that the best execution of this is to imitate the actor Mads Mikkelsen, as he portrays the character Dr. Hannibal Lector on the NBC TV show *Hannibal*. If you haven't seen the show, get the DVDs, especially the first season, and take a look, or check out the Youtube videos of it. In it, Mikkelsen appears wholly unemotional, and hyper-observant, as he takes in everything in a scene before him.

Mads' portrayal is suitably unemotional to elicit the hijacking effect, and mildly threatening in it's calm, controlled focus. It is also quite alpha and dominant in its demeanor, radiating a calm, controlled, all-observing and all-knowing mien. So rather than looking like some sort of emotionally-void mental defective, like the mother in the Stillface experiment, you look socially acceptable, if not socially exceptional – something which will be important when we discuss narcissist defenses to the hijack.

Since first discussing this online, I have had several people tell me that they have used the Hannibal Lector Stillface mien to great effect on narcissists they were dealing with. In many cases, just adopting the Stillface, and denying your narcissist the emotional feedback that they desire can leave them unsettled enough to begin avoiding contact with you. In my experience, combined with even a moderate amygdala hijack, the effects are nothing short of amazing.

Brashness

Brashness as a term encompasses a complex grouping of traits, including flamboyance, aggression, amusement, emotional detachment, combined with a colorful delivery designed to provoke amusement in the aggressively-minded. Not everyone can exude the quality of brashness, but if you can, there will be situations where the more of those traits you can pile together, the better the effect will be on an amygdala hijack.

It is a mien which can be particularly devastating when delivering conceptual hijacks to the narcissist which would normally elicit compassion and sympathy, were the narcissist a normal human being. One thing narcissists can acquire comfort from is sympathy. However the brash delivery, done correctly, exudes almost bemusement at the misery of the narcissist.

As we discussed, blogger Matt Forney has actually made use of a brash delivery combined with conceptual amygdala hijacks to promote his blog and acquire name recognition. He makes use of amygdala hijacks delivered in brash form, to stir discussion of his blog and gain name recognition.

However, one question has haunted me. It is the question of why the Stillface mien is so effective in some situations, while brashness works in others? I suspect the key to understanding this is an understanding of violations of expectations, and the priming effect they can have on subsequent amygdala hijacks.

Violations of Expectations

I believe that this likely amplifies amygdala hijacks powerfully, through application of a primal error stimulus that primes the ACC to activate unusually strongly. Once the ACC is active and operating at a high tempo due to perceived errors of expectations in the environment, it appears to become hyper-sensitive to further stimulation. Subsequent amygdala hijacks appear to lead the amygdala to call for aversive stimulus from the ACC, at which point, the already-activated ACC will then trigger an outsized neural alarm/aversive stimulus.

You can picture this in yourself. Enter a wrestling competition, and let your opponent pick your foot and trip you. You expected him to try, so while frustrating, it isn't really angering. Now try to walk to your office, and let some bonehead stick his foot out to trip you. Your fall will be much more angering, even though you let yourself be tripped in the wrestling competition the day before. The anger will arise, in large part, due to the violation of expectation. Now, you expect the idiot to recognize his mistake, and act contrite. What happens when he laughs at you? Again, a violation of expectation.

This might have evolutionary roots, sort of taking an animal which has noted that something is off in it's environment (error-stimulus triggered ACC activation), and making it hyper-sensitive to any subsequent amygdala-registered threats. Regardless, adding a violation of expectation seems to have a potent effect on the amygdala hijack. You can see this in action if you return to Matt Forney's hijacks of the feminist crowd.

Matt's hijack's bothered me for a while, because Matt was brash and aggressive, using vivid, and even profane imagery to trigger amygdalae – yet I had found that in person, the hyper-unemotional

Hannibal Lector Stillface Mien precipitated the greatest hijacks for me, while an attempt at a stimuli bombardment literally de-hijacked my narcissist. Why was this?

I have come to the conclusion that in it's own way, each presentation, be it Stillface or brash, is amplifying the operant hijack's effects, through the addition of a violation of expectation stimulus that primes the ACC to deliver a more powerful neural alarm/aversive stimulus when amygdala-triggered.

In the Stillface mien, the narcissist is trying to provoke you, and they are expecting a provoked, emotional mien from you, but you are instead providing a wholly different, unprovoked mien. In the narcissist's (and the Stillface baby's) mind, something is off. You will see this in the Stillface baby on the video, because his first expression is one of confusion. It is as if he is saying, *"Wait a minute...Something here doesn't make sense..."*

In Matt Forney's case, one expects written articles to be relatively unemotional. Additionally, he was saying things in his articles which the feminists innately expected should be eliciting shame and immediate supplication from him. The Feminists expected him to say such things meekly, and weakly, and to exhibit the type of mien which they could swiftly rebuke, and manipulate to elicit shame, supplication, and regret from.

Instead, he provided his anti-feminist ideas boldly, shamelessly, and with a brashness and amusement which they were not prepared to see. His writing style was a violation of expectation. As a result, their ACC began to light up as it flashed a weak alarm indicating some error of expectation was present in their environment. As it did, his amygdala hijacks hit, called up even more aversive stimulus, and in the presence of his violation of expectations, some feminists apparently found that their ACC triggered a panic attack that had profound physical symptoms, and disabled much of their higher cognitive function. That semi-coherent feminist warning about Matt's article is perfectly expected of one undergoing an amygdala hijack.

If you return to Nancy Hopkins, the MIT scientist who nearly blacked out over Larry Summer's calm description of how it was possible that men and women might have different cognitive abilities due to some different biological purposes, she was expecting that academic environment to be a specific way. She was expecting anyone who said such things to be ashamed of them, or at least obviously shame-able. Men were supposed to know to immediately defer to her, and nobody was to say anything freely, or without regard to how the politically correct crowd would view it.

When the President of the University said such things unashamedly, and asserted them as fact, she was hit by not only a sense of helplessness, and not only by the hijacking stimulus of spoken political crimethink, but also a very primal perception that within her environment, something was not as it was expected to be. If she were a baby, solely seeing the error in her expectations of the affects of others around her, and wholly absent the shock of the crimethink, I could see her, furrowing her brow, and looking as if she were about to say, "*Wait a minute, something isn't right about this....*" Of course, as the Stillface video shows, the next step is a total emotional meltdown, followed by a writhing convulsion, and indeed, that is essentially what we went on to see.

If you are familiar with the concept of r/K Selection theory operating in humans, as laid out in *The Evolutionary Psychology Behind Politics*,[1] you might notice something here. Under that model, there is a natural transition from r-environments (resource abundance) to K-environments (resource shortage) which occurs as resource consumption rises to meet, and then surpasses, resource availability. As that transition begins, and food is no longer freely available, r-strategists (abundance consumers) will begin to notice certain things seem "off," and events begin not occurring as they had in the past, as the K-strategists (scarcity competitors) begin exhibiting the less socially restricted, more aggressive psychology they are programmed to exhibit in K-selection.

Suddenly, individuals are no longer shame-able, and care less whether the crowd views them as good. Value/social signaling, common to conditions of abundance will recede as raw violence and competition becomes more common. In-grouping and aggression towards out-groups becomes normalized, while the tolerance (which functions as a confrontation-diminisher in r-environments), disappears. Things change from the r-model of society, in subtle ways which will innately violate the expectations of r-strategists. Suddenly, failing to behave properly can

---

[1]   Conservative, A. (2012). *The Evolutionary Psychology Behind Politics*. Macclenny, FL: Federalist publications

have real, Darwinian consequence, and such events can unfold quickly, to the tremendous disadvantage of r-strategists. In such an environment, where r-strategists begin noticing things are violating their expectations, it would not be maladaptive to see their amygdalae begin to freak out easier, with less stimulus, when things begin to look "off." Indeed, it could easily be the difference between life and death, since it could motivate them to flee to a more resource-rich environment, more in accordance with their reproductive strategy.

We know, that type of error detection will activate the ACC, producing a weak neural alarm due to error perception, and that the ACC is highly active during the stronger neural alarm designed to provide aversive stimulus due to things like social ostracization, envy of others with superior amounts of self-relevant resources, physical pain, and perceptions of unfairness (itself a violation of expectation). It is not out of the realm of possibility to postulate that one call for a neural alarm for error detection would combine with a second call for outright panic or anger, and each would amplify the other.

Judging by the accounts of the leftists mentioned in this book, this apparently culminates in humans by producing an innate behavioral response akin to that of a human possum – they promptly vomit on themselves, and then immediately pass out unconscious at their enemy's feet. It is also not hard to see the evolutionarily adaptive potential, among weaker animals that cannot compete violently, of such a reflexive, unconsciously-produced behavioral response when confronted with K-selection.

When I think of violations of expectation, of course, the first person who is brought to mind is the actor Gary Busey, who by his very nature, is a walking talking elicter of human error-detection stimuli, and possibly a master amygdala hijacker as well.[1]

---

[1] For an analysis and video of how actor Gary Busey, whether consciously or unconsciously precipitated an amygdala hijack, see : Conservative, A. (2013) "The amygdala hijack in action – a video example." <http://www.anonymousconservative.com/blog/the-amygdala-hijack-in-action-a-video-example/> (Accessed May 20, 2014)

Concentration Interruption and
Confusion/Error Detection

When you interrupt someone who is focused on a task, you are taking an amygdala which has prioritized one item, and forcing it to try to multitask for a moment, by scanning what you are presenting. This overloads an organ which is only designed to focus on one thing, and this overload can create feelings of frustration and irritation, all of which further stimulates the amygdala. These feelings can be greatly exacerbated if your interruption is confusing in some regard, likely due to triggering the ACC's error detection mechanism in a manner similar to violations of expectations. This is a highly cumulative hijack – whereas the first interruption produces minor irritation, the tenth can provoke a highly charged response.

I have not used this much myself, but I have had it used on me, by my narcissist, before I came to know what he was. I have since seen it used elsewhere. When I have seen this executed, the individual waited until the person they were attacking was maximally concentrating and focused. Apparently, as they were waiting for that moment, they would think up a question, but not one which could be easily understood and answered quickly. It would be a question which made no sense. As an example, if the person was working on troubleshooting a gas engine, you would ask, *"Is it the female one that's broken?"* Delivered just as the target is focused intently on a train of thought, that question forces the target to table his train of thought with hopes of answering your question quickly so he can return to his work, only to then wonder, *"What is the female one? ... And what does broken mean?"* The emotional response of the target will usually be to pause to answer, followed by a frustrated and pained expression, combined with an audible, *"Uuhhhh. ...Huh? What do you mean?"* By the tenth time this was done, the target would be quite perturbed, and usually insist that the hijacker leave the area, so he could work in peace.

The question would require much planning because you would have to prepare an excuse, to make it sound as if you just misspoke, or didn't know the term for something, so you used the confusing terminology you used. Maybe you meant the negative battery wire, or the spark plug connector, when you said the female one – you just weren't thinking when you said it.

The key in this hijack is to interrupt with a pointless question, and to make that question confusing, so in addition to irritating with the interruption, it triggers the error-detection/confusion circuitry of the ACC. I have seen one individual on whom this was done repeatedly, finally snap, and engage in a violent outburst that he couldn't control, complete with eye aversion, to try and rein in his overcharged amygdala. For a specific type of goal-oriented psychology, this hijack is devastating.

Frustration

This is narcissist 101. Partly due to envy of success, partly due to a desire to irritate, and partly due to a strange desire to see those around them unhappy, most narcissists will try to frustrate their targets at one point or another, by preventing them from attaining their goals. Usually they will get away with this for some time. For most people, the idea of a person ignoring their own personal aspirations, and instead devoting their entire life trying to stifle the aspirations of others seems so strange as to be impossible. Yet this is exactly the path that many narcissists follow.

Frustration can be engendered many ways. Sometimes is is done by distracting an individual just as they begin to focus on a task. They can introduce non-problems as if they need to be solved first. They can try to shift your focus to something unrelated to the task that you need to finish. They can talk endlessly, and act exasperated if you do not abandon your task to focus on them. They can accidentally screw something up, necessitating the whole project be redone from scratch. I have even seen my main narcissist act confused, and demand that everything stop so that everything can be explained to him. He would then act as if he didn't understand what he was told, introducing frustration just in trying to explain the task to him. If you are goal oriented, it is very irritating.

Again, many of these behaviors only make sense if you view them from the perspective of a narcissist. They want you irritated – more than anything. These petty irritations are the only way they can act out against you. When they demand that you explain something to them, feign an inability to understand, and then watch as you grow increasingly exasperated, they feel amusement – and that is as much

99

happiness as they can get, with their disorder. In their mind, it is funny that you think they are stupid, because they are actually in control, and amused at how stupid you are – getting all emotionally upset, directly because the narcissist is knowingly pressing these buttons in your head.

Two sets of techniques arise from this knowledge – one for if you are the attacker, and one for if you are the target. If you are the attacker, then you want to use the very tools the narcissist uses. Talk endlessly, and insist they listen instead of work. Accidentally screw up something exhausting that they just finished, and then apologize profusely. Demand to know what is being done, why, and then ask an endless series of inane questions about why that is important, the answers to which you will have great difficulty understanding. Find a problem unrelated to your objective, and insist it be solved prior to embarking on the real job. When somebody tells you that the problem doesn't matter, insist it does, and act confused when someone tries to explain how it doesn't. Finally act as if you understand and agree, then insist again that your problem must be solved first, because the whole project will fail if it isn't. Wait until somebody is just about to attack the job, then stop them, and introduce an obstacle to their getting started. Repeat as often as you can get away with it.

If you are the target, then you must understand that their objective is to irritate you by frustrating you. As with most narcissist techniques, their success depends upon your decency, loyalty, and desire to not cause any feel-bad in those around you. If you understand the game however, you can embrace the feel-bad, as you play the game better than the narcissist.

If you are the target, your counter-objective should be to evince zero irritation, and finish the project quickly and well, whether the narcissist likes it or not. When confronted with this I would send the narcissist on a meaningless errand, and finish the job in his absence. If need be, conceal your progress, and hide your work, so he has no idea until you are finished. Ignore him when he talks, and tell him you don't have time, then ignore his feigning of being hurt. Tell him that he is the only one intelligent enough to solve the meaningless problems he introduces, so he must do so himself, while you and the rest of the team handle the real job. Arrange for everyone to show up and work without telling him, and then act as if excluding him was just an oversight.

The key is to dehumanize the narcissist within your mind, hate him, relish seeing him frustrated and hurt, and understand that those emotions will result spontaneously from you not getting irritated at his games, and your finishing the project. Once you recognize that this game is purposeful, and that the narcissist's goal is to screw you over, you are freed to pursue your goals freely and do whatever you need to.

Disgust and Awkwardness

I have seen narcissists use these two negative emotions to try and stimulate the amygdalae of targets. One narcissist who comes to mind seemingly had a prepared routine about the name his wife had given to his genitalia and the reasoning behind it. As he went through this routine with an expression of glassy-eye'd, socially unaware, total focus on the subject, in front of women, you could watch the observer's eyebrows furrow, foreheads wrinkle, and wide eyes looking side to side at other observers, as if to see if they were getting this.

Again, as a narcissist technique, it depends on the politeness and kindness of the observers. Nobody would want to interrupt him to tell him that he was disgusting and revolting, and shouldn't be talking about that in polite company, let alone among women. Instead, trapped by their niceness and politeness, these victims sat patiently, suppressing their grimaces, and endured the awkward discomfort.

The narcissist, meanwhile would evince just the slightest glimmer of being pleased as he concluded his bit, I assume in response to the uncomfortable nods, defensive body postures, and befuddled stares he had precipitated.

I am not sure of the utility of this technique for the normal person, or how a narcissist would respond to the presentation of these stimuli to themselves. They might have reduced disgust tendencies, defusing the effects of that attack. I also would not present an awkward stimulus, as I assume the narcissist would save the information, to argue to associates later in favor of out-grouping you, as socially uncomfortable to be around.

I have never used these myself, nor do I recommend it, but I include it here for completeness, as it is one of the weapons I have seen narcissists deploy. It is helpful to understand how narcissists strive to stimulate the amygdalae of their targets, using whatever noxious stimuli they can find to present, so in that regard, you should file the information away.

Stress and Worry

Stress and worry are two potent tools that narcissist use to attack their targets. They are mainly effective due to the persistent nature of their stimulation of the amygdala. They are also two potent tools to use against the narcissist, but I would caution that you must use them a certain way. In order to be effective, you must constantly remind your narcissist of the negativity which is stalking them, but you should couch it as negativity in the present tense.

I have noted that narcissists seem well practiced in denying the significance of any future reality which is not yet upon them. Tell them they are going to be executed by the government in a week, and they will create a false reality in which they will escape before then, or the Governor will grant them clemency, and this will blunt the degree of amygdala stimulation. However tell them that they are now convicted, and sentenced to death, and the stimulus carries more of a factual, undeniable, present, in-the-moment nature, rendering it less amenable to being blunted by the imposition of a false reality over it. I assume the factual, definite nature of the delivery aids it to better penetrate the fog of vagueness the narcissist seems to view all reality through.

For the sentence to have maximal impact on their psyche, they must see the execution as a fait acompli. You must make it seem concluded by emphasizing the undeniable, immediate, factual aspects of it. If you wish to walk them through the stress of the execution, you would walk them through visualizations of what will occur, in the present tense.

The best things to stress a narcissist about are out-groupings in some regard, competitive failure against other people (preferably people they hate), abandonment, exposure, sudden life changes they can't control (loss of job, eviction, divorce, decreasing attractiveness or physical capacity due to aging, disowning by friends and family, exposure of their defect publicly, financial consequences, etc.), or the imposition of anything they seem to be using a false reality to hide from.

If what I observed in one of my narcissists is any clue, you want to develop several ways to subtly guide the narcissist's focus back to these subjects, and repeat this regularly, perhaps with questions about it (*"Have you seen any indication you are going to be the next to be laid off?"*), comments, (*"It's a shame to see how all the landlords are evicting poorer old people these days, just to get more rent out of the new, younger, more successful renters."*), or even by leaving newspapers laying around open to articles related to the stressful topics. (*"Dumping relatives in assisted living facilities the new rage among young people who want freedom."*)

As an example of how to execute this strategy, one narcissist I knew was told by a doctor that he should see a physical therapist to treat an old injury. His wife, ever the loyalist, stopped off at a local Physical Therapy Center, and picked up a brochure. The front part of the brochure advertised the Nursing Facilities at the site, while the second part advertised the Physical Therapy Services they offered. She placed this brochure on her desk, meaning to give it to him. Like most narcissists, he regularly went through her things, looking for intelligence.

Weeks later, after appearing strangely panicked for days, he blurted out in horror that he knew she was going to stick him in a nursing home. He had seen the brochure, and for days it was all he could think about. (Probably because if he had the ability, he would have relished sticking his wife in the nursing home). Had she known he was her enemy, she could have been dropping hints here and there about how he couldn't take care of himself anymore all along, and he could have easily been made even more panicked prior to the outburst.

Inducing Emotion

One thing I have seen narcissists do repeatedly is purposely induce negative emotions such as sadness, envy, fear, or frustration. My main narcissist would often tell stories of shows he saw on PBS, featuring nice little animals who struggled bravely against the forces of nature, only to suddenly end up experiencing some horrific fate, just as they seemingly overcame their hardship. Again, if you are nice, you feel it would be rude to interrupt, but interruption and ignorance is all these characters deserve.

If a relative experienced a negative event, my main narcissist would relish turning the subject to that, so he could recount it to others, in front of the relative. When doing this, it was clear that he was making a conscious effort to walk the relative through all of the unpleasant events which they were a part of. I can remember one time where a relative of his looked horrified, as if they were reliving the whole experience behind their eyes, as he recounted each agonizing part in excruciating detail. He looked delighted, and it was only after repeated attempts by observers that he was able to be forced off the subject – something he looked most displeased by. At the time it was one of those strange things he did, but in retrospect, it is now clear that this was purposeful.

When I have used this against narcissists, I would first find out the events of their life which left them horrified or depressed. This is easy, because narcissists love talking about themselves. Begin a conversation about the event, ostensibly to offer sympathy, but then recount each agonizing part of it to the narcissist, so they relive it, on the pretense that you want to understand what happened better, and are genuinely interested in them. Periodically ask emotionally relevant questions, such as, *"How did that make you feel?,"* or, *"What did you think when he said that to you?"* Emphasize the painful parts, by asking things like, *"Really, [such and such] happened to you?,"* or, *"What are the chances you would have something that bad happen to you – it had to be one in a million!,"* or, *"That must have been shocking!"* Although none of this would seem that devastating to us, these are exactly the sort of stimuli which so savage the narcissist that they have to retreat from reality, into a personality disorder of unimaginable awfulness.

When I do this, I make sure that the questions emphasize how bad it was, how sad it was, how awful the predicament is, how trapped they were by it, how permanent the negative effects are, how they can never undo the damage, how things like that always happen to them, how angry it must make them, how frustrating it must be, and I won't be afraid to laugh at how bad it all is, and how it could only happen to them, to introduce a violation of expectation. These are all emotional triggers, which set off those negative emotions that are so traumatic to the narcissist.

What I am really doing, is guiding the narcissist to re-experience the negative emotions from their own negative experiences, which they have adapted their brain to experience so strongly. By providing my attention to them as I walk them through those emotions, I am probably giving them some motivation to continue following that train of thought, as they are expecting some sympathetic climax to it all from me. That sympathy would give them a perception that they had manipulated me into being positively predisposed to them. Lack of sympathy, and especially laughter at such a climactic moment (such as amused laughter at how, *"Only you could have it so bad!"*) will deny them any narcissistic supply from sympathy, and really trigger their error detection circuits, even as it emphasizes the magnitude of the negative emotions they feel. It will also be extraordinarily traumatizing, as they will have endured all of that negativity for nothing, and you will be highlighting their inferiority on top of it all.

Although I have seen the narcissist use general stories of sad events which happened to outsiders to sadden their target, I think for that to work on someone, you have to have an empathetic soul, and a desire to not see bad things happen to others. For that reason I think general stories of sad events that happened to outsiders are probably not as effective on the narcissist. Far better are personalized re-visualizations of torments that the narcissist has suffered personally, combined with expressions of amusement that they have it so bad.

Droning, Monotony, and Pacing

I do not fully understand this yet, but it is a phenomenon I have noticed that is associated with several narcissists that I have crossed paths with. Some narcissists often drone on about boring topics, in a near monotone. Occasionally, I have noted a repetitive, rhythmic pacing to the drone, especially when listing things, as if they were metering their speech like a limerick. Not all do this, but I have known two who did, in quite a pronounced fashion, and both could leave you shut off mentally after just a short period with them.

I suspect they do this as a way of shutting off your amygdala's flagging function, and thereby depressing your central nervous system. Between the boring topic, the monotonal delivery, the metering giving it a very predictable, unsurprising quality, and the narcissist's depressed demeanor, your amygdala just gradually sees nothing of note and literally shuts down the brain. (Repetitive rhythmic chants are used in military training to shut off the amygdala's focus on, and awareness of the moment, making arduous, repetitive activities more physically tolerable through a sort of "brain numbing." One example would be chanting the, "I don't know, but I've been told... /I don't know but it's been said..." type rhyming chants while running.)

Whether this droning makes you more compliant around them, and less likely to notice how horrible a person they are, or whether they just get a kick out of slowing people's brains down and seeing people shut off, I have no idea.

To better understand this, imagine that you are in your front yard, target shooting exploding melons with an AR-15 and a nearly limitless supply of ammunition. A flying saucer comes down, and grey-skinned aliens jump out and run towards you, trying to grab you, to kidnap you. Your amygdala will go on high alert, in response to all of the intense, unpredictable, interesting, and frightening stimuli before you. It will suddenly focus on everything very intently, notice and remember every detail, and put the rest of your brain into high gear, as thoughts, observations, and decisions to act, fly through your brain at lightning speed. Your adrenals will pour out stress hormones which will increase your heart rate and blood pressure, your entire nervous system will go into high gear, your muscles will prepare to explode into action, and in that moment, you will feel energized and alive. It is the same physical feeling people get riding motorcycles, skydiving, snowboarding, jet-skiing, and raising hell with friends. We all know this physical feeling, and it feels good. You are alert, energized, and time can even slow down, as you drink in a myriad of stimuli in each moment that passes.

By contrast, when I would deal with either of the two narcissists that I caught droning, within ten minutes, I was in the exact opposite physical condition. After I left, an hour would seem to have passed like a minute around them, and the memory of that period of time would seem very similar to what one would experience from having been in a coma. After leaving, one would actually feel as if their brain had been numbed.[1]

---

[1]   In *Glimpse of the Devil*, Scott Peck wrote of one woman, ostensibly possessed by demons, who was visited by a priest to be assessed for exorcism: "*Several days later, the church sent a young priest to talk with Jersey. Later, he would tell me that Jersey had said something horrible to him–he couldn't remember what-and he had no other recollection of the visit.*" I can't say it wasn't the devil, but I can

A friend and I got caught by one such narcissist for a short period, and immediately after our escape, we blankly glanced at each other and, without saying a word, both broke out in stunned laughter at how exhausted and shut-down each of us looked – we didn't even have to say a word. I suspect the droning on about meaningless topics, in a monotone, and even adding a rhythmic quality to each listed meaningless item, gradually shut off our brains, until we both looked like we were walking zombies. As with most things associated with a narcissist, I suspect that they know that they are doing this, and probably have noted this aspect of the amygdala's manipulate-ability due to some altered cognitive experience of their own, produced by their own defective amygdala.

I've never spent time trying to develop the technique myself. I am not sure I even could, and am not even sure that being able to do it to a narcissist would be of much use. I only note the phenomenon here to bring the reader's attention to it, so they may be aware of it when they see it, and learn to guard against it by ejecting such a narcissist from their company.

---

say it could also have been amygdala manipulation by a master of the art.

Chapter Twelve

Further Notes on the Hijack - Bypassing Defenses_____

Your narcissist, if hijacked, will experience an uncomfortable sensation which is well described as pressure building up in their amygdala. They will first respond by expressing the traits of their personality disorder, all of which are a direct attempt to somehow diminish or release this pressure. When I would hijack, a secondary goal I had was to deny them any relief from this pressure, by preventing their use of the typical methods narcissists use to try and relieve or release this pressure. Usually these defenses boiled down to anger releases (rages), crowd-perception manipulations (out-grouping, ridicule, attention diversion, etc.), or internal perceptual modifications (reality denial), all of which would ideally be anticipated, so they might be countered appropriately. Generally, anger had to be forced to be stifled, crowd perceptions had to be controlled, and internal perceptual modifications had to be countered (through exerting control over focus, and logical analysis), all with prearranged techniques, kept at the ready. Properly done, this would maximize the amygdala melt-down produced.

The best hijacks are carefully planned, so I didn't try to do all of this on the fly. With time you can learn to exploit openings as they occur in conversation, but especially in the beginning, new students have to plan each hijack carefully, identifying the stimuli that their narcissist fears encountering the most, predicting how they will try to blunt the effect of the hijack, and then preparing a counter-measure which will negate any blunting effect of the narcissist's defense. If your narcissist is bad enough, and you get good at this, keep a few different well-crafted hijacks and counters in your quiver, and roll one out after the other. You should have a good chance of being able to reliably produce the "stroke."

Reality Denial

The first method a narcissist will use to try and blunt the effect of a hijack on their amygdala is reality denial. When preparing to hijack a narcissist, it is important that one eliminates any ability of the narcissist to deny the reality that will be presented to them. Construct an argument or two linking the hijack to an undeniable reality, such that the narcissist can't deny what you are about to present to them. If you were going to point out that they are a failure, you must have one or two clear failures to throw in their face should they try to deny it. If you were to show they are a liar, you must have one or two clearly established cases where it is clear they lied, and others accept that as reality. A hijacker must tie the hijack into some undeniable reality, and refuse to allow the narcissist to fall back into a false reality. You should also make it clear that the reality will be known and recognized by all, and cannot be hid from the crowd.

Laughter

Laughter is another tool narcissist seek to use to distract and diminish the effects of a hijacking stimulus. It isn't normal laughter though. It is a loud, boisterous, fake laughter designed to try and make it appear that what you are saying is so ridiculous the only response one can have is to laugh. Joe Biden used this in the 2012 Vice Presidential Debate with Congressman Paul Ryan. Whenever Ryan began to quote specific statistics showing how mismanaged the government and economy were under the Obama administration, Joe would look at the ceiling and laugh his fake laugh as a way of distracting people from the substance of Ryan's factual arguments. It worked for the most part, because instead of focusing on Ryan's withering factual assault on the state of the government, people only remember Joe laughing. Even though Joe looked like a tool, he managed to prevent Ryan from creating an inarguable factual case for that administration's gross incompetence and ineptitude.

The key to defusing the laughter is to refocus the narcissist's amygdala on an attack which is designed to make the laughter itself stimulating to the narcissist's amygdala. Point out how the only time they laugh is when you are quoting facts that are obviously correct, so each bout of laughter could be used to show where their logical case is weakest. You can also use an amygdala hijack to associate the laughter with aversive stimulus, which will often stop the laughing ploy.

Had I been Paul Ryan, in the debate with Joe Biden, I would have paused, and looked shocked, to draw attention to myself, and away from the laughter. Then I would have calmly made note of the fact that I had only ever seen laughing like that two other times, and in both cases it was in a family member of mine with extreme Narcissistic Personality Disorder. I might have looked confused as I said it to draw attention to the idea that Joe seemingly was exhibiting a symptom associated with a personality disorder. From there, I would have looked shocked again, and then made explicit note of any instance which which would hijack his amygdala.

To do this, I would have locked eye contact, invaded space if possible, made physical contact by grabbing his forearm strongly, and looked surprised as I recounted one of them as evidence of his brain problem. In Joe's case, he has a lot of instances which are embarrassing, potentially out-grouping, or which might be able to be couched as indicative of some form of mental illness. Grab one, preferably one which which will trigger his amygdala strongly, and hit him with it. *"When you said Obama was an amazing candidate because he was a clean, articulate Black man, it was because you devalue Black people to assuage your own insecurity! Wow! And then you spoke about Indians being in all the 7/11's. You tell yourself they are inferior to you, because they are just service people at convenience stores. Wow!"* If Joe was a narcissist, that is out-grouping right there, and it will hit his amygdala dead on. If he had the disorder, he would probably not even look too closely at what you said, or try to refute it logically. He would just get emotional and angry as his amygdala began to activate.

Then I would have thoughtfully and sincerely added (while lost in thought) that, *"I'm very impressed that you are so functional, while operating under such a mental handicap."* From there I would make note that I should not have discussed his mental health publicly on national TV, apologize, and deliver another apology for discussing his mental health to anything else he said. I would strive to deliver it all so fast, that he would be unable to react, or interject until I had unloaded all of that. When he then tried to deny it, I would just say, *"No, you're*

111

absolutely right – I should never have discussed that publicly – I'm so sorry." Were Joe a narcissist, he would not have laughed again in the debate, because his amygdala would have linked the laughter with the negative stimuli of exposure, out-grouping, diminution of status, violation of expectation, and frustration which followed it.

The Agony of Rules

Societies and groups of people establish rules. Rules are designed to constrain human behavior into a set of predictable, and established norms. Rules may exist as legal statutes, or merely the rules governing some social organization. Narcissists will seek to use the rules to constrain the behavior of others, while simultaneously avoiding such constraint themselves. This is maddening, since most of us tend to structure our behavior according to right and wrong, and trust that this will comport with the rules, where necessary. This means that since we do not always structure our behavior according to the rules, we are left vulnerable at times to being called out on rule violations. Narcissists know this, and exploit it, because it is what would most frustrate them.

The real problem arises when narcissists manage to seize some form of authority within a group, allowing them to determine what rule violations will be enforced, and on whom. In my experience, this is difficult to fight, because it is a form of warfare that is alien to normal people, who are designed to function socially based on subconscious social impulses imbuing their behavior with a morality and pro-sociality that manages itself.

There are only two ways to effectively fight against this. One is to rigorously attack and out-group narcissists whenever they try to associate with any group you care about, at the outset of their association, before the troubles begin. Dealing with the narcissist is not the time to be guided by rules designed to be fair to all, or to behave chivalrously. Dealing with narcissists is nothing more than an immoral, naked power struggle. Either you treat them decently, only to see your group ultimately corrupted and destroyed by small minded petty dictators, or you run them off at first sight by any means necessary.

The second way to fight is, if the narcissists have managed to take over the group, simply leave, form a new competing group, and trust that your group, being run more decently, will eventually make their group irrelevant.

You can try hijacking them, making meetings unbearable, and using the rules of the group to attack them, but in the end that is a power struggle, the outcome of which will be determined by how thoroughly the narcissists have solidified their position, and the lay of the terrain on which the battle is fought. If you can win that way through hijackings, politics, and rule policing, great, but recognize that you will always have the ability to walk away, and start a new group.

Above all else, never allow any of them to feel as if their actions have bothered you in the least. You are in the fight solely to bust their chops as much as possible, and after you are done enjoying that, proceed seamlessly to plan B, to continue their irritation. Their sole objective is to see you miserable. No other victory will satiate them, and that is the one victory that you can fully deny them, simply by not being bothered.

Stifling the Urge to Anger

Another strategy narcissists use is yelling and aggression. The goal here is to bully people into accepting their false reality, by making resisting it unpleasant, due to the yelling which will occur if they resist. A secondary goal is to begin a large yelling argument with you, which will distract the narcissist, and you, from the hijacking stimulus which they need to ignore. In my experience, rage is a pressure relief valve that the narcissist uses to release the pressure within their amygdala. If you can hijack them, and prevent the use of rage to vent their amygdala pressure, you can force them to let the pressure build, and eventually that will likely produce the stroke-symptoms.

In my experience, expressions of rage are best countered by going hyper-unemotional, stillfaced, Hannibal Lector, and looking at them as if they are puzzlingly crazy. Your expression would say, *"What is wrong with this person?"* One would also lock an unblinking eye contact for further effect. Then I would redraw their attention to the hijacking stimulus. Note that rage is often seen as one approaches the narcissist's meltdown point. It is usually a last ditch effort to parry a devastating pain that has almost come to its climax.

For most narcissists, if you stimulate the amygdala enough, you will precipitate a violent response, as they will need to vent that pressure, and a violent response will be the only way to do it. But what would happen if they couldn't vent their amygdala that way? In that case, by blocking the amygdala's pressure relief valve of violence, you would be increasing the pain the narcissist would feel several-fold, and you could eventually precipitate the stroke-like symptoms.

In my experience, it is possible to prevent the use of violence/aggression by a narcissist to vent their amygdala, through a few different means. Note that as you prevent them from venting the pressure which builds up in their amygdala, you make the hijack more painful for the narcissist. They need to be violent, they want that outburst, they have to have that fight, to relieve the pressure, and get everything off their chest. Box them in so they can't engage in it, and it will only make things more frustratingly painful for them.

Here we will look at some techniques I have seen narcissists use to bottle up the amygdalae of their targets, so they cannot act out violently.

Conflict Avoidant Facial Expressions

One way I have observed narcissists deliver amygdala hijacks, without eliciting violent responses, is to deliver the hijack while wearing an oblivious, conflict-avoidant facial expression.

One narcissist, known to me through a friend, loved to attend happy festivities, and covertly trigger violent arguments. Sometimes these were funny to watch, sometimes not so much. In one case, there was a nice get-together, at which this narcissist proceeded to trigger an unpleasant turn of events, using the conflict-avoidant facial expression to suppress any violent responses among his brothers, who were the target.

By way of prior explanation, he and all of his siblings held their deceased mother in an almost unbelievably high state of worship, almost to the extent that it would seem the relationship may have been in some respect pathological. Referred to almost always by her formal first name, "*Virginia*" was always portrayed as strangely beyond any reproach. Her status was even on occasion used to win arguments, on the sole basis that she might not have approved of something. One brother once induced almost immediate supplication in another merely by saying accusatorily, *"What would Virginia think of that?"* The brother who supplicated did so almost out of reflexive, conditioned fear, rather than logic.

On the day in question, everyone was having a great time, bantering back and forth. During a brief lull, this narcissist suddenly decided to interject, matter of factly, in front of his brothers, that he was certain that his mother had an abortion. He then adopted the conflict-avoidant facial expression, and stared out into space, as if lost in thought over the prospect. There was a long, 20 or 30 second period of totally dead air, as the statement, and its implications, gradually sank in among all those present (namely, that their probably half-brother wasn't at the gathering because their slut mother, had their half-brother killed behind everyone's back, so she wouldn't have to deal with him). Bored wives immediately perked up, obviously most curious at what was about to happen, as the narcissist's brothers looked at each other in offended shock, their amygdalae growing energized at this wanton assault on their mother's honor.

Suddenly, one blurted out, *"That's ridiculous!,"* to which the narcissist responded unemotionally, with the conflict-avoidant facial expression, that he remembered her taking him on the train to it, and waiting in the office while she had it done. It went back and forth, The narcissist's brothers angrily denying the possibility of it and looking for the fight, and the narcissist, wearing the conflict-avoidant, clueless facial expression, sticking by his guns, and delivering his responses, asserting it was true. The happy mood had ended, though this one didn't devolve into a fight.

This hijack was actually prepared ahead of time. About ten days prior, this narcissist had blurted this out to to another relative, who had confusedly told me, unsure why the narcissist thought he would care. One aspect he noted was the narcissist's very careful examination of him and his response, after dropping the bomb. In retrospect, that narcissist was carefully preparing for the family gathering, and his ultimate destruction of it. (Even narcissists prepare their hijacks carefully.)

The conflict-avoidant facial expression is very similar to the stupid smile adopted by the old comedian Stan Laurel (you can google his image to see his expression). However when I have seen it used, it

115

had less of a smile, and more of a detached, unaware, unemotional quality, partly due to it being delivered with glazed eyes, as if lost in thought to the point of being unaware of one's surroundings. To adopt the expression, you must first drive your eyebrows as high as you can. Then pinch in your dimples, if you can, and draw your cheeks outward, stretching your mouth as widely as you can, while pushing your upper and lower lips together, and rolling them inward so as to minimize the amount of red lip visible to onlookers. Let your eyes glaze over a little, so it appears as if you are lost in thoughts, and not really aware of what is going on around you. Tilt your head slightly to the side, and let it hang, so you appear as out-of-it as possible. There is a reason Ollie never did a number on Stan like Moe did on Curly. The conflict-avoidant facial expression Stan wore was nothing like Curly curling up his nose and looking angry, as he bounced up and down and made funny noises in anger.

I have seen a couple of narcissists use this expression when they do something they realize should anger other people. I have no idea why so much knowledge among narcissists is so standardized. It is as if they have some sort of textbook. Today, if I see this expression, I assume I am looking at a narcissist, and if they are doing something irritating I will assume it is purposeful, and they are trying to avoid the consequences of it, and force me to bottle up my amygdala. I will also use this myself, to deliver a massively triggering hijack, while forcing the narcissist target to hold in his anger.

Humor

Being good humored as you poke fun at someone, and deliver amygdala hijacks, is an excellent way to force your target to bottle up their anger. This is kind of like ridicule, but with a good-natured flair that would make the narcissist fear acting out against you, less they look angry and unbalanced. This has the additional advantage of getting the crowd laughing at the narcissist, which for some reason, is a stimulus which almost universally enrages narcissists beyond all measure, and sets them up beautifully for amygdala hijacks.

116

Continue to a New Subject

A second method narcissists will use is a subject change. The subject change is an actual attempt to replace the hijacking stimulus in their brain with another, less bothersome stimulus. This will often be combined with an attempt to produce emotional upset in you (something narcissists find pleasurable), often by changing the subject to one which you find emotionally upsetting. An example might be, *"I'm a liar? What about when your dog died last year, and you didn't even care about it. You're insensitive."* The best defense I have found to this is to go Hannibal Lector, and guide the subject back to the lying, preferably by pointing out how his change of the subject only reinforces what a sleazy liar he is, followed by an actual, undeniable example of a lie he told.

There are times when you will drop a bomb on a narcissist which they will want to respond to immediately, to refute. These can be criticisms of their competence, allegations of untrustworthiness, assertions of their pathiety, etc. If you drop that hijack, the narcissist will experience an immediate need to refute it in the eyes of all present. I first noted this technique for stifling that in an old roundtable discussion, and have since used it myself with excellent effects. When preparing your hijacks beforehand, have a subject change that you can implement immediately, to move away from the hijack you drop. The subject being changed to should also be inherently amygdala flagging in some way, so as to draw attention away from the previous subject/hijack.

The narcissist's amygdala is often operating at the outside of it's functional envelope. As an example, in a political debate, if you drop a hijack asserting that the narcissist is immoral, immediately, before they can respond, move on to a castigation of something different, such as an assault on their leadership abilities, using a specific policy failure to focus attention. In the narcissist's mind, their amygdala can't hold all of that negative information at once. As you move on, you force them to leave standing the first hijacking stimulus, and in their eye, that negative information is still hanging out there, and established as truth among the crowd, by their non-response. This preys on their mind, since the fundamental trait of the narcissist is an inability to confront negative stimuli – especially that which is established among the crowd.

However, if they return to the hijack, to try and refute it, they must actively return to a piece of negative information – something their brain is programmed to dislike. Furthermore, returning to "old" material reeks of try-hard, making it appear that the statement may be valid, if they are so concerned with it that they will return to it.

On the other hand, if they let it stand, it would appear as fact, more so to the narcissist than anyone. Narcissists define their reality by what they can get the observers around them to believe. If a narcissist can get everyone to agree on some false reality they conjure, which makes them look incredibly superior, they will be in a state of bliss, believing this new reality fully, even if that false reality is wholly ridiculous. In contrast if you really want to make a narcissist go mad, get everyone around them to agree on a falsehood which portrays the narcissist badly. It will drive them crazy, and depress them even more than it would if it were true.

Here, by placing a hijack in the public record, and moving on before the narcissist can refute it, you create a most painful conundrum for the narcissist. They can go back, focus their mind on a negative assertion about themselves, call the attention of others to a negative piece of information, possibly confer some element of veracity on it, and risk having it accepted by others even more strongly. Alternatively, they can leave it be, and let a negative assertion which they will think about compulsively, remain unchallenged in the public record of their discourse.

For the narcissist, it is an unsolvable conundrum which drives them nuts.

Admit Nothing, Deny Everything, Make Counter-Accusations

Another strategy is to deny that your hijack was intended to make the narcissist upset, or even accuse the narcissist of being overly sensitive. Acting as if they are being weird, and there is something wrong with them, is even more triggering. Or feign confusion over their sudden outburst, why they would be so angry, and the inappropriate nature of their emotions. Their frustration in being unable to explain to you why it was bothersome can be even more entertaining.

Narcissists know there is something wrong with them. I suspect many times, they are not certain whether people notice it or not. By

118

acting as if their outburst is a sign of weirdness, and mental defectiveness, you would frighten the narcissist over whether they will be exposed as a mental defective. This fear can force them to stifle their emotions, even as every fiber of their being is screaming out in agony, begging to be allowed to rage uncontrollably.

A lot of this depends on the environment within which they are being hijacked, however. Portraying them as weird and overly emotional in front of a crowd will have much greater effect, and force them to stifle their emotions far more, than doing it in an isolated environment.

Regardless, when they blow, and execute a narcissistic rage, it is with the assumption that you will grow emotional opposite them, allowing them to vent their stress while making you emotional. Your emotionality is supposed to render you unable to castigate them over their emotionality, and even help conceal their weirdness. If you suppress your emotions, lock eye contact, and calmly portray them as out of control, hyper-sensitive, and overly emotional, while portraying your hijack as grossly misunderstood, you will drive them insane.

Make Attacking You Like Attacking the Group

Another technique narcissists will use to try and counter your assertion of reality is to make adherence to reality out-grouping within the group, so the group will force adherence to the narcissist's false reality. If the narcissist can force the group to espouse their false reality, then they can immerse themselves in it, and shield themselves from further discomfort.

This will involve some way that your position is contrary to a moral or belief which the group holds as sacrosanct. If you insist on everyone getting a piece of cake, and they want to deny certain people cake, they will ask if you really want to take cake out of the children's mouths. If you want everyone to pitch in equally to pay for a vacation trip, they will ask why you are forcing the poor among you to pay as much as those with more, who could better endure the hardship of a vacation expense. You get the idea. The narcissist's goal is merely to try and have the group fortify the false reality that they have already constructed to serve their own ends, and make it so that to continue to adhere to reality, you must create a schism between you and the group's

119

moral center. The answer is to find a way that adhering to their false reality renders them unfit for the group.

Narcissists fear being out-grouped, or viewed negatively by their social circle. Since their psychology defines its reality by the beliefs held by its group, if the group views them negatively, they will be forced to view themselves negatively, which, as we have shown, is among the most painful agonies you can inflict upon them. It is like the opposite of a false reality which portrays them as perfect.

For this reason, if you can deliver your hijack, while couching it in such a way as to portray it as associated with the group (ie a group consensus, or group-held belief, or a group-moral which runs counter to something that the narcissist is known to have done), you can make opposing the hijack (and you by extension) out-grouping. This will force them to quietly endure the hijack to maintain their group affiliation, while stifling their urge to rage, to release their anger.

Chapter Thirteen

*Pressing Buttons, Amygdala Focus, and the Cumulative Effects of Amygdala Stimulation*___

One of the keys to understanding amygdala activation in the narcissist, is to realize that that if you focus someone normal on something which is unpleasant to think about, the response will be bothersome, but not physically rending. In the narcissist however the same stimulus can, with repetitive exposure, be grossly disabling.

I picked this fact up from my favorite narcissist, after noticing that he always seemed to eventually steer conversations with people to ideas or occurrences which bothered them. He would rail about the evils God did to the religious, remind a brother of some failure he had which cost him an opportunity, tell an animal lover about some horrible thing he saw happen to an animal, or just call attention to a depressing fact in his target's life. In a moment of unguarded honesty, he once referred to this as *"pressing people's buttons."* Buttons pressed could involve fear, sadness, worry, anger, frustration, unfairness, envy, hatred, disgust, awkwardness or any other negative emotions or experience.

In retrospect, in his head, people had things which depressed them, irritated them, scared them, worried them, angered them, or were just unpleasant to think about. If you called these topics to the attention of their mind, they would think about them, and in their mind, a button would be pushed calling up the assigned emotional state. What people don't realize is that in a psychology like the narcissist, where the mind is hyper-sensitive to negativity, the effects of this can be cumulative over short periods, and maybe even long periods. When I executed that first hijack on my narcissist Bob, I made use of this aspect of their psychology

I knew several things about Bob. One, he had experienced a horribly unfair event, which worked to the immense benefit of a man he loathed. Two, he hated women. Three, a woman he knew had experienced the same event, in exactly the opposite way – where he had suffered immeasurably, she had enjoyed a tremendous success. Four, he would likely never again regain what he had lost in his horribly unfair event.

I knew Bob "pressed buttons" at this point, but I viewed it as a mark of his patheity and wholesale impotence. To me, being relegated to such a pathetic means of merely emotional attack was something one should be ashamed of. And yet, here I was, using this stupid, seemingly pointless technique against him.

I began talking to him about his problems. I focused him on them. I made him think about the people who had it easy and succeeded from his suffering, the woman who enjoyed her success, how he would never get back to where he had been before his failure, and then I brought him right back around to the beginning and repeated the process. I marveled at the magnitude of his irreversible situation. I acted astounded at how he could never go back to how things had been. I noted how lucky the woman was to have everything go perfectly, when he was so devastated. I laughed at how only he could have it so bad. Before long, he announced blithely that he was "having problems." Within minutes I was in a car with him, driving him to the emergency room as he showed all the signs of a full blown stroke.

He got so angry that parts of his brain began to shut down, just as if they had been deprived of oxygen by a blood vessel blockage. I assume that as he became enraged, his brain began a period of extreme hyperactivity, and this consumed oxygen and nutrients faster than they could be replenished. As his brain exhausted its reserves, parts of it shut down due to lack of fuel, just as if he were having a stroke.

After a night of observation and a full battery of tests, doctors proclaimed that they had no idea what had happened. After I repeated the process with him a few times, Bob no longer would even go to the emergency room when the "stroke" began, choosing instead to lay down until the symptoms passed. Eventually, he stayed away from me entirely, though he never once postulated that the amygdala hijacks I did were what was triggering his episodes. He apparently preferred that everyone think he was just prone to periodically "stroke" out, to letting everyone know that he suffered from this vulnerability.

In my experience, the single most important thing to understand about the amygdala hijack is that the effects of each amygdala stimulation are cumulative over the short term, and maybe even somewhat over the long term. Administer that first shock, and you will activate the amygdala, and fire off a set of neurons which can only take so much firing. With each subsequent activation due to a hijacking stimulus, these neurons enter an even higher gear, and burn their rapidly diminishing nutrient reserves even faster. Each hijack you deliver takes a little more out of a gas tank that only has so much to give, and when you've exhausted it, wild things can begin to happen. Narcissists may even begin to panic as they realize that they are approaching the point of no return, and this adds to subsequent stimulation.

This horror is the worst thing the narcissist can imagine. No failure in life, no moral transgression performed, no horror of reality, can compare to the magnitude of terror produced by realizing that their victims have found out about this mental pain that they experience, and now their victims can inflict this pain upon them, using nothing more than words.

Chapter Fourteen

Hijacking on the Fly _____

In my experience, executing a live amygdala hijack on the fly, is too complex an endeavor to be done extemporaneously, except in the most fortunate of circumstances. Hijacks usually will require preparation. You need to dwell on them. You need to imagine yourself, as your narcissist. What are you hiding from? How could someone force you to confront that? How would you avoid being forced? How could your avoidance be overcome? What is a piece of undeniable evidence which would shock you into touching reality, and which would make denial impossible? How could it best be presented, to maximize the shocking, trapping effect, offering no room for any intellectual escape? How could you, as your narcissist, be tricked into trapping yourself? How would you try to counter a hijack? What would you tell yourself? What would be the most shocking counter to your counter? What will they be expecting, and how can you violate that expectation, to make them feel as if they can't predict what will come next?

I imagined playing it out in my head. I imagined catching mine in the false reality. *"You just said this, and now you've changed it because you knew the previous version wouldn't stand up to reality! You must know you're lying, because you just adjusted your argument when you got caught in a lie! You know! And now I know, that you know!"*

To do all of this, you have to know your narcissist. You have to know what they will say to deny the reality they fear, what they will argue to support what they say, and how to tear it all apart around them, in a way that makes them look stupid to everyone else. Know how to point out to the people around you that the things the narcissist demands costs the group, in a way which should out-group them.

125

When the narcissist stumbles, and begins to grow flustered, you need to have prepared yourself to strike the slightly amused and interested, yet unemotional Hannibal Lector facial expression, as you lock eyes, and closely examine the signs of emotional stress on their face. You need to have prepared ways to push them further. Invade their space, release information they don't want exposed, lay hands on them as if chummy to make them uncomfortable, shock them with the amygdala hijack, and do it all as if it is perfectly normal.

Most of all, you have to prepare yourself, so that you know that your narcissist's outsized emotional response is a sign that the hijack is working – it is a sign that their amygdala is turned on, and they are flailing to avoid what comes next. It is the sign that you should press forward, unemotionally and steadily, in the direction you were going when the hijack began.

There is a learning curve to hijacking, and I didn't do this perfectly from the start. But as I practiced it, I saw what worked and what didn't on my narcissists. Eventually I gradually learned to control their brain and mood, in the same way that they, for so long, controlled my thinking and mood. As I traveled that path, I found myself subconsciously devaluing their worth, and feeling ever less need to treat them politely, as if human. The farther I went down that road, the less affected I was by the narcissist's emotional head-games.

Unfortunately, the amygdala hijack can only be really understood by doing it to a narcissist. One can highlight how the narcissist rages uncontrollably, and how the fierce strength of the emotional sensations behind that can be turned on, as if by pressing a button, if you understand what precipitates it. You can explain how this neurological upset is so powerful that it is physically rending to the narcissist. You can recount cases where narcissists have described feeling as if they are going to black out, or throw up when it is done to them, and even cite cases where people stroke out. But in the end, you have to actually do it to a narcissist, and watch as all the rage, all the vitriol, all the hatred melts into a dejected pile of physical sickness, apathy, and depressed horror that can't think, reason, or even control their own brain or body. I have watched a narcissist compulsively look at the floor, unable to make eye contact, visibly sick, and marveled at how he relished making everyone around him miserable, until he was placed in that state, using nothing more than words, expressions, and body-postures. His evil and noxiousness were only to be rivaled by his weakness, pathiety, and vulnerability.

It is a potent power to have, in a relationship which often consists of only absorbing abuse, and dreading beyond measure, your encounters with the narcissist. But it is not without risk. Narcissists are crazy to begin with, and if you keep trying to break their neurobiology, you may succeed, and push them fully over the edge. If that happens, anything is possible.

So it is not recommended that you do this, or forget to be vigilant in protecting your safety if you do. Visualize your narcissist's reactions, recognize how the hijack controls their behavior, and even prepare hijacks for use, should you need them. You can even walk up to the line, and begin to stimulate their amygdalae, and watch the reactions. But only use this technique in its full-blown form if you really feel as if you will not be able to survive if you don't. Any more widespread use could result in precipitating a violent outburst – and given how crazy the narcissist is to begin with, it will almost certainly be an attack you will never be able to predict, or protect yourself from.

Chapter Fifteen

How to Manage a Narcissist to Make the Relationship Nice_____

This will be a very short chapter. Most narcissists are unmanageable over the long term in personal relationships, or at least they have proven so to me. The only viable management style I have found is to get as far away from them as possible.

This conclusion surprised me, because as I unraveled my first narcissist's psychology, I thought it would make it easy to control him. Within his brain was the neurological equivalent of a dog's choke collar around his neck, in the form of the amygdala hijack. All I needed to do was snap the choke, by making him confront reality, each and every time he got out of line. Soon, he would be a good little narcissist, not raging, and not trying to poison the people around him, or make everyone unhappy. Maybe I could even train his brain to become normal. However, it didn't work. In fact, if anything, he began to redouble his efforts, under even deeper cover, and go even more crazy beneath it all.

The problem is this. Narcissist's need freedom from all unpleasantness. Worse, they are programmed to hate everyone, so the only thing which will make them relaxed and copacetic is you being miserable and tortured. As long as you are not miserable, and are un-tortured, that itself is miserable to the narcissist. Without you, miserable and tortured, their world cannot be perfect and free from all unpleasantness. If you correct them to try and bring them in line, they only get more panicky and desperate to see you miserable. I never found a way around that, and I'm not sure there is one, outside of donning gangrenous latex prostheses and makeup, hiding some rotting meat under your clothes for smell, and fooling your narcissist into thinking you are mortally ill, at death's door, with Leprosy, all of the time.

Even worse, narcissists are programmed to operate below the radar. If your narcissist ever does suddenly get nice and caring, you need to watch out, because there may be a nasty surprise lurking about, and they are trying to guide you into it with niceness, and are only happy at the thought of you, about to fall into their trap. Maybe they have sabotaged your brakes, maybe there will be some ant pesticide in your scotch, maybe they are even about to try to kill you in the garage.

Now, even if you decided to accept a certain level of misery, and give the narcissist the high degree of control that they want, you will still have a problem. Narcissists are unbalanced neurologically, in much the same way an addict is. The more suffering you endure, the more they will need you to suffer, to get their high. Worse, with every agony, you will feed their ego, and everything from their arrogance to their sense of omnipotence will grow. The more they get away with, the better they will feel, and the more they will feel they can get away with in the future. The more they feel they can get away with, the more they will do. It will be a vicious cycle only ending in your demise.

Additionally, there is another facet of the narcissist to consider. Joanna Ashmun wrote extensively based on her experience with narcissists.[1] Her work is brilliant, and will describe most narcissists to a "T." One of her observations is that narcissists are weirdly competitive about insignificant details – not in the way an athlete is competitive, but in the envious way a sneak and a cheater is competitive. Whatever strange detail falls under their attention, from the type of shampoo you use, to the number of tools in your workchest, to the type of shoes you wear, will be viewed competitively, and enviously. Of course that is an outgrowth of an amygdala, hypersensitive to any negative stimulus, no matter how absurdly minor. Once the negative information is noticed, that amygdala will blow it out of all proportion, to the point that it cannot be ignored, and must be addressed in some fashion.

However it is also related to the fact that the narcissist doesn't actually know what real happiness is. Since they never get happy, I suspect that they have come to the conclusion that happiness is a competition that everyone engages in to acquire the most trappings of happiness. They further assume that if they win, everyone around them will be envious and angry as a result (like they would), further

---

[1]   Ashmun,   J.   (1998)   "Narcissistic   Personality   Disorder" <http://www.halcyon.com/jmashmun/npd/index.html> (Accessed 20 May, 2014)

enhancing their drive to "win" the competition. So they try to make sure they have all of the trappings of happiness equal to, or better than, those around them. This produces a desperate, all consuming drive to win this competition mechanistically, even though they don't seem to enjoy true emotional happiness from the trappings like everyone else.

Now the thing this raises, that you need to consider, is that in my experience, as narcissists age they are suddenly thrown far behind in this competition, by their own measures. Old narcissists look around, and see a world of young happy people, with their whole lives ahead of them, enjoying the use of young bodies which function perfectly, as they pursue a plethora of seemingly limitless opportunities. By comparison, the old narcissist is old, unattractive, their body is broken down, their opportunities are gone, their life is coming to an end, and none of that will get better. On top of that, as a narcissist, they are even more miserable emotionally to boot. To the narcissist, they are old and broken, and everyone else is young and happy, and that obsession will make it impossible for them to have all of the trappings of happiness, or even come close. This will tend to produce an even increased desire to drive those around them down, and make everyone as miserable as possible, so everyone else will have less relative happiness, and the narcissist will not be so bad off in the competition.

As they age ever more, this envy becomes a desperation. It combines with an older, more neurologically enfeebled brain, less capable of hiding their true nature and less motivated to do so, to produce an extraordinarily noxious character, bent on making everyone miserable, and not even attempting the vaguest pretense of being even mildly normal. Altogether, this will fuel everything, from rages you will not be able to imagine, to a spark of insight in the narcissist, that if only you were just a little sicker and less happy, everything would be so much better.

Things will go downhill rapidly from there.

I recognize some readers are attached to their narcissists, and leaving them behind may seem cold, and unkind. You want a way to make the relationship work, and make your happy objectives the same as the narcissist's, so you can both work together to achieve the same happy ends. The problem is, you are projecting your goodness on your narcissist. Your narcissist is not human, like you, no matter what you think. They are basically like a Terminator robot, programmed and designed to destroy your happiness and make you miserable. It is all they are programmed to do. While they execute that programming, they never get happy per se, but rather are miserable and angry constantly. That constant misery and anger is written into the very operating system of their brain.

If you give up on managing them, and separate from them, they will be just as miserable and angry as they are now. Nothing will change for them – it is how they are designed. Indeed, if they cross paths with you later, they will only get more angry at your happiness. If you leave, and never see them again, they will be exactly the same wherever they are, and maybe even less angry than if you maintain contact.

Best of all, you can find happiness. A world of narcissist-free beauty is out there. There is no downside to leaving your narcissist behind, if you can do it. It doesn't hurt the narcissist, no matter what they will say, and it may even be nicer for them. For you, it will suddenly render this beautiful world of beaches, and mountains, and grassy meadows, and streams, and butterflies, sublime.

In short the only way to really manage a narcissist is to get as far away as possible, whenever possible.

Now, if you can't, all is not lost. In the coming chapters, we will explain strategies and concepts which will hopefully help you interact with your narcissist, if you can't get away immediately. However these are not solutions, and they will not solve your problems in the way that a full and permanent separation will. They do hold the promise of making your life considerably easier, though, until you can negotiate the full break you deserve.

Chapter Sixteen

_____

*So You're Going to Break Contact*_____

The only answer to dealing with narcissists is to break contact, and not deal with them.

There are different ways to break contact with your narcissist. How you do it, and how much you stimulate your narcissist's amygdala depends on your circumstances. I advise a minimum of conflict and amygdala stimulation, wherever possible. This is because the consequences of amygdala stimulation can be severe, and you usually cannot easily undo them once amygdala stimulation is performed. By contrast, the consequences of not performing amygdala stimulation as you break contact will usually be milder, and if need be, more easily ameliorated through the subsequent application of amygdala stimulation, should it prove necessary. You can always stimulate an amygdala later if you want, but you cannot always undo the consequences of amygdala stimulation, once executed.

As an example, imagine that you are leaving a job under a narcissist boss for greener pastures. Here, I would make a conscious effort to avoid stimulating the boss' amygdala, especially if you need to give a certain period of notice before leaving. This may even preserve the ability to get job references later.

Of course you could always strut in one morning and say, *"Everyone here sucks, this job is crap, I hate you all, and I am so happy to be going off to a much better job somewhere else, while you tools are stuck in this miserable craphole!"* However from that moment forward, the sight of you will trigger the narcissist's amygdala, and they will feel driven to make your life miserable. Specifically, this statement will trigger your narcissist boss' amygdala in three ways which are significant.

First, you are going off to a better job. Narcissists need to be the ones heading to greener pastures, while everyone else is left behind. If you are going somewhere better, your boss' amygdala is going to be on fire, because in his mind, he is just a loser, trapped in the hellhole that you are happily leaving behind. The only way he can feel better about that is to drive you into the ground, every chance he gets.

Second, you are criticizing the boss and his work environment. That is also amygdala stimulating for him. Who are you to imply that he is less than perfect? For that, you will need to be punished.

Finally, you appear happy to be going. Happiness in others is, all by itself, more than enough to trigger a narcissist's amygdala. Nobody is allowed to be happier than the narcissist. That will have to be fixed, and it won't be by a narcissist who decides to make himself happier than you. It will be by a narcissist who makes you more miserable than the narcissist.

Much better would be to go to the boss, and explain how your mother is sick, and you are dreading the responsibility, but you need to get a less successful/more onerous job, closer to her, so you can spend all of your free time taking care of her. (I'd have no shame about lying outright to a narcissist, since I really don't view them as human.) This explanation works well because it negates the three primary amygdala triggers highlighted above

First, to the narcissist, you are miserable. Narcissists want those around them miserable. If a narcissist boss sees events making you miserable, he will actually feel as if he has had a stroke of good luck. It is almost as if he were blessed with a surprise vacation from the responsibility of having to make you miserable. I have literally known narcissists who would have reflexively entered an almost giddy mood in direct response to this news. Once in that giddy mood, they would accept bad news happily, and exhibit a much higher tolerance for general amygdala stimulation, before entering rage mode.

Second, you are only going because events have forced you to, so the narcissist won't feel as if you are criticizing him, or his work environment. Third, you appear to be moving down the ladder, and back to a lower position. This will prevent the boss from feeling jealous of you for cruising off to greener pastures, while he is left behind going to the same old job.

By telling this lie, your last thirty days at that job will be much easier, and you will even preserve a future job reference, should you someday need it.

Things change when your association with the narcissist is social, and when the narcissist can choose to make contact with you. Here, normal human politeness and kindness will usually be an enemy.

In my case, I had reached a breaking point with my narcissist, Bob. I needed him out of my life, but unfortunately, I was among the last of his social contacts to eject him from their lives, so he was resistant to ejection.

One of the stranger things about narcissists is how they can just show up, as if nothing happened, after epic blow-outs. You can say the nastiest things to one, tell him you will never talk to him again, he may even vow to kill you, and then he will just show up at your house the next day, as if nothing happened, with a six-pack of beer, and asking if you have anything to eat. To a normal person who wants to re-establish contact, the blow-out would stand out in their amygdala as a highly negative piece of data, indicating that re-establishment of that relationship would be a non-starter. The narcissist, however, doesn't register that data similarly. They probably deny it to some degree, form a false reality where it never happened, and experience subsequent amygdala relief. They probably also don't prioritize it as unusual, due to constant feelings of rage and hatred making it seem less unusual. As a result, they can show up as if nothing happened – and may even believe that nothing did happen.

By this time I had begun to understand the amygdala hijack, and could reliably pull it off, so that is what I began doing. Basically I hijacked him every time I saw him, until he couldn't stand my presence any longer. At one point, he was staring at the ground, visibly sick, saying, *"I can't do this face to face stuff any more – I'm going to write you a letter."* I never got the letter, but he did eventually stop trying to make contact with me.

I was lucky in some ways. In being the stupidest of my friends, family, and acquaintances, I was the last to cut Bob off, so once I ejected him, we had no mutual acquaintances. Many cases end up being complicated by such mutual acquaintances. There, you must tread very carefully. What will undoubtedly happen is that your narcissist will try to poison everyone in your social circle against you, often with blatant lies and extraordinary tales of your moral degeneracy. My advice here is to never involve your mutual acquaintances, beyond correcting any untruths they raise with you, while expressing brief disappointment at how the narcissist has lied.

Everybody has an amygdala, and those amygdalae are constantly scanning the environment, and setting the mood for how those people perceive the world, and the people in it. As a result, subtle emotional perceptions are constantly attaching themselves to you, in the eyes of your friends. If every time you greet a friend, you open your interaction with a hilariously funny joke that makes them double over with laughter, they will begin to see you and smile reflexively, wondering what crazy thing you are about to say. Their amygdala is scanning their environment, and when they see you, their amygdala will recall the funny encounters past, and begin to prepare them for a funny encounter presently by putting them in an appropriately happy emotional mood.

Conversely, if every encounter is drama filled, with negativity in the form of stories about the psycho who is stalking you, and the horrors you endure, a lot of that negativity may begin to attach itself to you in their amygdalae. Pretty soon, your friend may not even be aware of it consciously, but seeing you will not precipitate a smile, but rather a subtle bracing for whatever vicariously experienced horror comes next.

For this reason, your sole focus should be on being so nice to your friends, and helpful to them in their lives, that they will all wonder why the narcissist doesn't get along with you, and whether the problem may in fact be with the narcissist.

But never, ever drag them into the negativity you experience with the narcissist, or force them to vicariously re-experience the drama that you hate so much.

Because of the potential for social upheaval I also advise people to avoid unduly stimulating a narcissist's amygdala when possible, as a way of avoiding the battle before it begins. This means avoidance and evasion, rather than direct, open confrontation. If you don't want to spend the weekend with them, don't explain to them that you don't like them, and you are pissed off because they did something awful, so you are cutting them off. Invent an innocent excuse for why you can't make it, and create several go-to excuses, should they try to engage you in the future. Avoid them whenever possible, and be pleasant when it's not. And try to never have an argument in front of others.

The problem in going to war with a narcissist is that the narcissist has no rules. To the narcissist, what the group believes is, to them, "the truth." If the group believes they are bad, then they will endure the narcissistic injury of being forced to confront their own noxiousness. But if the group believes you are bad, then they can avoid the agony of the narcissistic injury, and actively define you, an enemy, as tangibly bad, which makes them, by relation, noble. To the narcissist, this goal will justify anything, from the most blatant lying, to the most devious social manipulations.

Imagine a husband and father, whose father in law is a malignant narcissist. If he opens a war, he is not only a threat to the narcissist's happiness. He is a threat to the narcissist's very perception of themselves as good – something so vital to the narcissist that from childhood, they will express the most damaged thought patterns, and endure the most dysfunctional life imaginable, just to try and protect it.

The narcissist's first play will almost certainly be to try and out-group his son-in-law with the family, either as an offensive move to attack his enemy, or as a defensive move to blunt any future such attempt by his son-in-law directed at him. That will mean splitting his son-in-law from his wife, the narcissist's daughter. Because losing is as panicking to the narcissist as death, he will be capable of stooping to any level – even levels normal people could not imagine.

He could create perceptions of an affair, to split his daughter from her husband. He could try to get his grandchild to allege molestation. He could poison himself mildly, invo0vle the police, and leave a bottle of the poison in his son-in-law's house, to be found by his daughter. Or he could just lie to everyone about everything, and before the husband knows it, his reputation in the family is buried under a pile of lies so deep, even he wonders who he is. If his wife is naive to the ways of a narcissist, and trusts her father, the outcome could be far worse, and his family could be torn apart.

The point is, when you are mired in a social circle, and especially a family, there is little upside to opening a war, and a whole lot of negativity which can flow from it, and attach itself to you and your life. Your best bet is avoidance and evasion, combined with an aggressive campaign to in-group yourself with everyone in the social circle. Be the guy who gets along with everyone, and who helps whenever he can. Bring the beer to the get-togethers, and make everyone laugh.

Sometimes, you will have no choice, and war will begin whether you want it to or not. In that case, I would be blisteringly nice to everyone, involve no one in it, and learn to amygdala hijack the narcissist at every opportunity, while trying to make the hijacks as unobvious to observers as possible. I would strive to make it so that when I attended a function, the narcissist would not be able to be in my presence, without experiencing an uncontrollable narcissistic rage that would make the narcissist appear crazy and emotionally unbalanced. However, in the course of all of this, never, ever, let yourself get emotional in front of other people, or appear emotionally upset yourself. I would also go into full documentation mode, as described in a later chapter.

If it comes to war, you will have to accept that your social life will be a roiling turmoil. As a normal person, you will never go to the lengths that a narcissist will, nor will you stoop to the tactics that they will use. But you can make it as miserable for them as it will be to you, and maybe even a little less tolerable, given the sensitivity inherent to their malady. If that is enough, and the battle can't be avoided, then you will have to do what you have to do.

Chapter Seventeen

Avoiding Conflict _____

If you have not yet locked horns with your narcissist, your first goal should be to avoid a war, if possible. To do this it helps to understand why narcissist's target certain people. You must first understand that the narcissist is miserable. Their brain is trapped in a mode that causes them to experience constant envy, insecurity, and anger. Certain individuals will set off these emotions like fireworks in their brain, and when those fireworks explode, the narcissist will feel driven to act out, and target the offending individual.

So what sets them off? It can vary, but usually it will be any sort of image which makes them feel inferior in some way, which reminds them that they are not the best individual at everything, or which reminds them they are not the happiest person ever. If your narcissist can't find love, and they see you and your spouse snuggling under a blanket with hot chocolates, on a cool fall afternoon, on the swing on your front porch, that will trigger their envy and insecurity. Why should you have love? They are nicer than you, they are prettier than you, and they should be the one with a loving spouse, living a Hallmark moment. It's unfair. So they will get angry and decide to make it fair, by making you miserable. To them, their actions are an expression of their morality, and their commitment to fairness and equality.

Are you younger? Richer? Happier? More successful? More respected? Better looking? More well liked? Do you have a nicer car? A nicer house? Do you laugh a lot and have a joyous demeanor? Do people light up when you come into a room, but roll their eyes when the narcissist shows up? They notice that, and it makes them angry because in their mind, you are just manipulating everyone into liking you, and worse you are doing it better than they are. It is not fair that you have so much good in your life, so they are going to do something about it, because they are principled, and you are undeserving. They will not let that unfairness stand - they will actually tell themselves that their willingness to act out to make you unhappy is a sign of their principled and moral nature. Other people might buckle down and endure such an insult as your flouting your happiness and likability openly, but not the narcissist. They will deal with it, and make you pay, no matter the consequences to themselves.

Once that initial bridge is crossed, you see where it goes. Now their amygdala is in high gear, and ready to rage at the smallest of stimuli. Meaningless things will pop up, the narcissist will decide they don't like *"that"* about you either, and their amygdala begins to shift into an even higher gear, and rage at even smaller things. They will look at the pretty landscaping in your front yard, and get angry that you force the neighborhood to look at such an ostentatious display. You'll bring a delicious cake to a neighbor's soiree, everyone will love it, and you will have done that purposely to both show up everyone else as inferior, and crassly manipulate the host into liking you. You are just so mean and immoral, and it is all so unfair. Something has to be done.

If you can avoid standing out, you can avoid trouble. Keep a low profile, don't openly let others know how awesome your life is, and don't make too big a deal about how happy you are. If you break those rules, you may set yourself up to be a target for any narcissists in the area. Some may ask why bother avoiding trouble, if you have to live like that, and it is a valid point. This book is only about options – the choices are yours.

Narcissists can act out unpredictably, however. Some may endure an insult from one person, and then look for the person that they think they can most easily get away with acting out against, to blow off steam on. Remember, every narcissist behavior is an attempt to vent pressure from an overloaded amygdala. You can best avoid being vented upon by trying to be the most universally liked person in your group, or the most powerful, so the narcissist will fear alienating the group, or incurring your wrath, by attacking you.

You may periodically experience an outburst, despite doing your best to avoid it. Narcissists have damaged amygdalae that are unduly sensitive to any negativity, even the imagined or recalled – and that stimulus may be wholly unrelated to the time frame when they experience it. The main one I knew most intimately was prone to quiet interludes, during which he was apparently ruminating on some humiliation from his past. As he ruminated on these ancient slights, his amygdala grew more agitated, he grew more angry, and Lord help whoever he happened upon immediately after such an interlude. He would be in a state of extreme irritation, and looking for someone to lash out against. If you experience such an outburst, I would advise to ignore it, and go on as if nothing happened.

I know. That seems strange to us. If we get angry, what made us angry is a tangible thing, and it needs to be resolved before we let go of the emotion. If someone makes us angry, we don't just forget about the insult if they ignore our anger – we get even more angry. But we are not narcissists.

The strange thing about narcissists, is how detached their emotional life is from anything you are familiar with. Imagine that you had spent your entire life barely containing epic levels of rage and hatred, and that you have hated everyone all of the time. Since you have always reflexively tried to act like your relationships were normal so as to fit in, one outburst can be easily forgettable. After an outburst, you would merely tell yourself that for one moment you let out what was inside, but now it is contained again. You would then say to yourself, lets all just go on smiling, as if nothing happened. So it often is with the narcissist.

They can release amazing amounts of narcissistic rage, only to turn around shortly thereafter, and act as if nothing happened. In truth, by raging they have actually unburdened their over-pressured amygdala, and now that it is back to a normal level of irritation, they can return to suppressing their rage out of sight, and acting normal (which in truth, is all they ever do).

Of course, ignoring it offers a couple of advantages. If you endure a narcissist rage and ignore it, it will make you look magnanimous and astonishingly even tempered to outsiders, and other members of your group. Should the narcissist try to turn them against you in the future, you will be unusually well positioned to repel such efforts. In such a situation, showing everyone that you are not the angry one is an important opportunity.

Second, not responding aggressively may allow you to avoid having the narcissist fixate on you. If you respond aggressively in return to their rage, this can lead to further rage episodes, as the narcissist begins to fear that you have "found them out," begins to feel as if you two have a problem, or just begin to enjoy having rage exchanges with you. But if you act as if nothing happened, the narcissist is denied the rage they were expecting you to exhibit, and they are probably made mildly uncomfortable by that violation of their expectation. In such a case, the storm will often pass, and calm weather will almost immediately return, sometimes shockingly fast.

There are different ways to cope with such a rage, without getting angry or emotional yourself. George Stephanopolus spoke of Bill Clinton's epic rages in the White House. According to Stephanopolus, he initially found them very emotionally unsettling, but he eventually learned to tell himself that Clinton was not raging at him, or anything he did, as much as he was raging through him, to blow off steam. According to Stephanopolus, visualizing the rage as an explosion Clinton vented, which harmlessly passed through him, helped. Once he viewed them that way, he was able to endure the rages, and when Clinton came back later as if nothing happened, he had a semi-logical explanation for why the rage he endured hours before didn't have any perceptible consequence on their relationship.

Personally, I would amuse myself at the display, and laugh to myself inside, thinking that this nut-job is so crazy that after this wild display, he's just going to come back and act as if nothing ever happened. Imagine shaking your head to yourself and laughing - just don't actually do it. Use the sheer scale of the narcissist's malady to draw amusement from episodes which would otherwise be quite bothersome, and you will exhibit the perfect affect, and be positioning yourself beautifully for future encounters.

I can't stress how much easier your life will be if you can stay off of your narcissist's radar, or how much more irritating your life can get if you end up in an open confrontation with them. If you are off their radar, they are a minor irritation. But if you end up in a full-on war, then your entire social life can end up a roiling turmoil of angst and anger. Avoid the battle if you can. The bottom line is, even the most vicious fight with the narcissist can't wound the narcissist anymore than the misery that they carry around constantly does, each and every day of their life.

Chapter Eighteen

Confrontation With the Narcissist

There will be those readers who have a narcissist with whom some form of conflict already exists, and with whom avoidance of the battle is not an option. You will have three options, namely, appease, attack, or escape and evade.

I have heard postulated a fourth option - that if you could confuse your narcissist, and leave them not knowing whether you were for them or against them, that you might be able to prolong the early phase of the narcissist relationship, where the narcissist tries to manipulate you with concessions into thinking that they are normal, so you form a relationship with them. I see a few problems with that theory.

First, I have never heard of anyone actually doing that. I suspect that narcissists will either sense that they have won you over, and begin their abuse, or sense that you are not an easy target, and cut their ties in search of a controllable abuse sponge. If this strategy was possible, I am certain that somebody, somewhere would have written a manual on how to do it. I classify this strategy as I would the martial artists who use internal "Chi" energy built up through years of meditation, to harden their chests, so swords can't penetrate them. You will always hear some guy who says it is possible, and some may even claim to know somebody who could do it or have seen it done, but invariably you will never be able to confirm it yourself.

The other problem is, what kind of relationship would this be, even if you could do it? It is natural for a normal person to form an emotional bond, and then, on auto-pilot, derive pleasure spontaneously from being nice. Introducing a person to your social circle, who is ostensibly nice, and who you then periodically have to abuse to keep them nice seems counter-productive to maintaining personal mental health and sanity. Additionally, the whole relationship isn't really a normal relationship. Rather, it is as if you are manipulating a robot to act nice, when that robot doesn't really have the same nice feelings inside which normal people have.

This is really the crux of the problem in interacting with the narcissist over an extended period. Recent research has shown that narcissists express positive affect in response to the sadness of others, and narcissists with some degree of psychopathy or Machiavellianism (ie. many narcissists) express negative affect in response to the sight of people expressing positive affect (happiness).[1] What that means is that narcissists get happy when they see the people around them sad, and many also get sad when they see the people around them happy. Lets look at an example.

You walk into a celebration, where everyone is dancing, laughing, and joyously reveling. You get in the mood, and pick up a party horn and a drink, and begin laughing and making noise with everyone else as you dance to the beat. The narcissist is different, though. Forever on the outside, the narcissist looks at that group, reveling and happy, and immediately compares it to the all-pervasive depression and rage that they always feel, and suddenly the narcissist feels like a loser, and begins getting angrier and more frustrated, even as they pretend to be happy on the outside. Pretty soon that anger turns to action, and next thing you know, you have a party where the women all flood out of the house with the children, as the fisticuffs begin inside due to the argument the narcissist got going among the revelers.

Now imagine you enter a funeral for a dear relative, who everyone loved, and who suffered greatly before they died. Everyone is sad and despondent over the loss, and it is only natural that you will tend towards moping too – in that scene you aren't going to see much to be happy about. By contrast, the narcissist enters that room, looks around, sees everyone crushed, and suddenly he doesn't feel so bad about his

---

[1]   *"...individuals high on narcissism, primary psychopathy, and Machiavellianism experienced positive affect towards sad emotions"*
Also,
"...primary psychopathy and Machiavellianism were associated with experiencing negative affect towards happy expressions."
From Wai, M., Tiliopoulos, N. (2012). The affective and cognitive empathic nature of the dark triad of personality. Personality and Individual Differences, 52, 794-799.

own situation. He is on top of the group, and he will begin to feel happy, even as he mimics sadness. In this paragraph, I actually stole the phrase doesn't *"feel so bad,"* from a narcissist I knew, who on hearing of another's crushingly debilitating medical condition, responded, *"Jesus, Dave. You know I hear about how badly your* [major medical incident] *went, and suddenly I don't feel so bad about my* [medical condition]." He actually sounded giddy as he said that. They genuinely enjoy the suffering of others, and researchers can even detect it in testing.

This is your real problem. It is tempting to project your psychology on the narcissist. It is tempting to imagine logic running their psyche. If you try to do that, you demote the misery they create, to a mere symptom of some underlying disorder, easily ameliorated with some palliative therapy. Suddenly, you begin to wonder, *"Hey, if I can just work around that disorder, then I can ameliorate the symptoms. Then I can have that same loving relationship with the narcissist which I have with other people in my family. Then we can all be happy together!"* This is made worse by the narcissist's periodic imitations of normalcy, each of which you instinctively see as the normal niceness you would do, motivated by your pleasure at seeing people happy, rather than the Machiavellian manipulations of a character who feels relaxation and satisfaction when he sees misery and unhappiness.

It is a painful realization, that the narcissist is not savable – I know, I made it myself, just as you eventually will. The upside is, you and the narcissist can be happy, just not together. If you stay together, one psychology that needs everyone happy, and one psychology that needs everyone miserable, then somebody is going to be miserable. There is no way to bring them over to your side – you are just incompatible. But part ways, and both of you can find the happiness you need, just in different places, preferably, far, far, apart.

However, if you can't break free completely of the narcissist, just yet, then you still have the three aforementioned options to deal with a narcissist, namely, appease, attack, or escape and evade

Appeasement

In my experience, long-term appeasement is a losing strategy. However, short-term appeasement can have short-term utility in managing a narcissist.

In appeasement, you approach the narcissist with an understanding of the origins of their condition. View them as a robot, with a sensitive amygdala. Stimulate the amygdala, and you get rage and fury. Gently assuage the amygdala, by ameliorating their stress levels, and you get a more copacetic response. They may even offer concessions to keep you around, to feed their ego some more. Alternatively, you can distract their amygdala, and focus them on other things, to keep their amygdala from experiencing negativity, which can also keep them manageable. The real goal is trying to guide the amygdala to avoid their freak-out. This is not ideal – it is akin to having a heroin addict in your house, and periodically breaking out the needle to give him a shot, just to keep him off your back. But it can buy you a brief reprieve over the short term.

A big problem is, over the long-term, the narcissist's underlying need to see you miserable makes a part of long-term appeasement the requirement that you never be happy, and often be sad. For this reason, I view appeasement as a strategy strictly suited to short term use, and preferably use which involves deceit, so you can feign unhappiness, rather than actually experience it.

If you have to give a narcissist boss thirty days notice before leaving for that great new job, use appeasement, and tell them how unhappy leaving makes you. Describe how awful the situation you are going to is. And never, ever, click your heels as you walk out of their office. In family relationships, you can try periodic appeasement to avoid tantrums, and in social circles, you can use it similarly to avoid confrontation, but I would advise including a deceptive element which indicates that you are miserable. Thus if a narcissist rages because you won't do "X," say you really want to, and it is killing you that you can't, but some uncontrollable circumstance is preventing you, and making you unhappy. Explain how much easier things would be for you from your perspective, if only you could do what the narcissist wants, and tell them how frustrated you are.

The real problem with long-term appeasement however, is that I think it makes the narcissist's problems worse over time, and renders the narcissist ever less manageable. In truth, I appeased for quite awhile with my main narcissist, before I figured out what he was, and he only got worse as I did. I am guessing many reading this have a long history of using this strategy themselves. It is natural, if you have someone you think is normal and loyal to you, to try and keep them from freaking out by being nice to them.

A big indice I had that something was very strange with my narcissist came from an incident when I finally reached my breaking point, lost my temper, and let him have it. After the interaction, I thought that would be the end of our relationship. The next time I saw him, he not only acted as if nothing was wrong, he was nice to the point of phoniness. Puzzled, and thinking he was now going to be nice, I was nice in return, and very quickly he became despotic and the raging tantrums began again over every minor amygdala stimulant. I acted cruel to him in response, and suddenly he was nice. It was very puzzling at the time.

What I suspect is, as you appease, the narcissist adapts, like a drug addict, to the niceness. Like a drug addict, they suddenly need ever more niceness, just to feel normal. Eventually, you could treat them like a pharaoh, with fanning palm fronds and peeled grapes, and they would begin freaking out over the speed at which they were being fanned. Even if you could properly calibrate your fan speed, eventually, they would feel so omnipotent, and so entitled, and be so prone to epic freak-outs, that no normal human could possibly stand their presence.

Basically, you should visualize the application of niceness and appeasement as being akin to giving a heroin addict a shot of heroin. For a short while, your addict will become manageable, but very soon, you are almost guaranteed that he will get worse. For this reason, I eventually recognized that no relationship with this type of individual could ever be tolerable for any length of time.

Attack

If you don't have the ability to escape, your second option is attack. Here, you approach the narcissist with an understanding of their condition, and you hit that amygdala with all you've got. As we've discussed, this is a risky strategy. If you have a narcissist, you've seen the sputtering rages which emerge from nowhere, in response to stimuli you didn't even notice. Find that amygdala, and punch it purposely, as hard as you can, and that sputtering rage can turn into a murderous spree by an out-of-control nutjob.

Plus, I have seen how having an amygdala, severely over-activated, over a long period, affects the narcissist over time. They will begin to break down, grow ever more panicky, and ever less capable of rational thought. This is only a strategy for those who are either willing to take the risk of violence, or capable of defending themselves, should it emerge. You will also need to be epically paranoid, all the time.

Again, as a long term strategy, I think this fails. At best, you will end up with an ostensibly cowed nut-job, who harbors great hatred for you, and who is probably plotting against you behind your back to gain revenge, either legally or illegally.

For those wondering, I have seen no indication that you could condition your narcissist with amygdala hijacks to act normally. I actually prefer calm environments, so when I first discovered the hijack I did not do it consistently, preferring to roll it out in response to bad behavior. There was no improvement, and eventually I just rolled it out continuously until my main narcissist could no longer deal with me.

The real problem with attack is that narcissists are often called *"grievance accumulators,"* probably because their faulty amygdala flags everything affecting them adversely as an epically massive attack on themselves, and thus they remember each instance strongly. Additionally, the anger it produces needs direction to make them feel better, so they will find someone to blame for the amygdala irritation.

As a result, they hang onto grievances far longer than most people, and they often act out on them, without warning. Since the narcissist is a snake in the grass, acting out never consists of a challenge to show up at the local boxing ring, for 3 rounds, under Marquess of Queensberry rules. Rather it consists of sneaking into your house when you are not home, and spiking your food. If the narcissist attacks, they will try to do so in such a way that you will never even know that they did, let alone be able to prove it.

This brings us to the final, and ultimate strategy in dealing with the narcissist. Since it is the best option, it will be given its own chapter.

Chapter Nineteen

Escape and Evade

Escape and evade are really two strategies, with the same goal, but we will treat them as one – getting as far from the narcissist as possible whenever you can. Escape is a total break, and it is the optimum strategy. Don't go for a half measure if at all possible. Evade is more for situations where you are trapped, and you can't escape, but you want to maximize your happiness all the same.

I view these not only as the most effective of long-term strategies, but also the most easily couched as moral to those in the tunnel. I know that many reading this will still feel emotionally attached to their narcissist. Your narcissist is damaged, he is hurt, and you don't want to hurt him more, but you need your life back, and moreover, you have reached a point where you can't even be in their presence anymore, (if you are not at that point yet, either you don't know how sublime a narcissist-free life is, or you haven't known your narcissist long enough – either way if given enough time, you will eventually get there).

That tendency to humanize your narcissist is normal, and I was there. The starting point of your journey is an emotionally bonded relationship with someone who you feel is just like you. The end point is truth – your narcissist is little more than an evil robot, programmed to try and destroy any chance you have of happiness. You are somewhere between those two points, which will usually entail your emotional bond making you view your narcissist as somehow human, and deserving of at least some measure of kindness. Meanwhile you view the aberrant behaviors as symptomatic of a malady that afflicts the narcissist unfairly, and prevents him from being nice to you, as he would want to, were he not afflicted.

If that is where you are, escape and evade is your best option morally. It does not entail the bowing before evil which is what appeasement really is. Nor does it entail the rank sadism which is required of those performing the amygdala hijack. Even I, knowing that the narcissist is pure evil, don't like doing that, or the drama which it entails.

By contrast, escape/evade is quite moral. The narcissist will be miserable wherever he goes. He will bring gobs of misery with him in suitcases and trunks, clouds of it will engulf him as he walks, and he will even make some more on the spot to fill in any voids wherever he may land. When you banish the narcissist from your life, it is not as if you are hurting him by suddenly making him miserable. It is not as if he was going to feel good with you, and you are punishing him by keeping him away from you.

He was going to be miserable, all along, right there beside you. He was always going to rage uncontrollably, right beside you. You are only sending him somewhere else, to experience that exact same misery and throw all those rages.

When you do eject the narcissist from your life, suddenly the world around you will become delightful again. You will make your small part of the world a better place. You will create happiness out of misery, and carve a small corner of the world into a beautiful oasis of happiness for you and the people around you. I cannot communicate to you how once the narcissist is gone, the sun's morning radiance will warm you to your core, how a cool spring breeze will invigorate your energy, or how the smells of nature will fill you, and make you want to breathe in the entire world. If you grasped that, you would realize just how immoral it would be to keep the narcissist around.

Now, how do you escape and evade? It depends on your circumstances. Whatever you do, I would try to employ appeasement to whatever extent it is possible to minimize conflict, provided the end result is as much distance as can practically be created between you and your narcissist. It just makes it all easier.

Escape and evade plays differently depending on how you are connected with your narcissist. Different relationships require different means of leverage to create the requisite space needed to be able to once again extract some enjoyment from life. Lets look at some cases.

Children

We will begin with the worst possible scenario. Your child is a narcissist, and you are legally obligated to take care of him until he is grown. I don't have all the answers for you, but obviously this is going to be an evade type of scenario.

From what I saw with Bob, he consciously used noxiousness to get his way, and it often worked. I can recall myself once imploring an associate to just give him whatever he wanted, so he would shut up and leave. I remember Bob flashing a small, almost imperceptible smile. I have no doubt that was acquired in childhood. Somewhere along the line, he acquired the behavioral pattern of being noxious to his family, until they gave him what he wanted to get him to go away. I can't imagine enduring the agony of having to parent that type of individual, and I am even more horrified to imagine a nice child forced to grow up around a creature like that.

The bad news is your child is broken, and it is almost impossible to fix what is causing the problem. I feel terrible saying that, but I have your ear for this brief moment, and this is not the time to mince words. Kids come out of the womb with a certain predisposition that nobody can control, and for whatever reason, far beyond your control, your child is not amenable to a reciprocal loving relationship with family members. Rather he or she is a robot which is programmed to perpetually destroy your life, your spouse's life, and the lives of your other children, at every opportunity, to attenuate their own natural, innate, bad feelings. I don't know if you can process that, but I would beg you to try. I have seen four great people, who were in such a circumstance with family members who were narcissists. All four gradually wore down and died, due to medical conditions that I suspect they would not have gotten had their systems not been continuously worn down by the stresses of close interactions with this evil, in the form of their children.

It is tough to describe the physical effects of long term exposure to a narcissist, but they are not health-inducing. Bob had so constantly stimulated the amygdala of one of his brothers during childhood, that after decades of not having any contact, the brother actually appeared emotionally traumatized, just by bumping into Bob for a few seconds at a family gathering, decades after his last encounter with him.

When you experience that level of psychological trauma, your body releases stress hormones. Stress hormones are designed to get the body through stress by turning off any biological process that is not necessary to immediate survival. By doing this, they free up energy and resources which were going to be used to build the body up for later, and allow that energy to be expended immediately, to get you through the stress.

If you are about to be eaten by a lion, it is helpful to mobilize every last bit of energy available, to help you escape. There is no point in building up more cartilage, so your joints function well later, if you are about to be eaten now. Nor is there sense in devoting energy to fighting that flu virus you caught, if such energy is better used to keep you alive right now.

However, such stress responses are designed to be transient. After the threat passes, the stress hormones recede, and the body will experience a rebound effect, whereby the processes which were shut off rebound into even greater activity than they had experienced before, and after a short while, the deficit of future fortification of your system brought about by the stress is rectified, and you are as good as new.

The problem with the narcissist is that they know how to stress people's amygdalae, in such a way that this stress hormone response will occur. They do it fairly constantly, and as a result, they create a fairly permanent stress state, where your body begins to stop worrying about fortifying it's systems for the future, and each unit of energy becomes devoted solely to making it through the present. Even when you are not actively dealing with the narcissist, your brain knows what is coming, and it maintains the stress state. Eventually, you will break down physically, because you will never be fortifying yourself, to repel future adversities you encounter. If just one cold virus hits, and you have no reserves, you will regret it.

If you are looking at spending a decade or more under that level of stress, as you raise your child, and then even more time, interacting with them as an adult, you will cut decades off of not only your life, but also that of your spouse, and any other innocent children you are raising. Bob's brother is clearly not well served to have experienced that level of stress in his childhood, or to have been conditioned to have such a major stress response as an adult, to little more than a chance encounter for a few seconds.

The problem is you can't escape until the child reaches adulthood, so what do you do? The key is to create oases of time in which you know you will not have to deal with the narcissist – the longer the better. If you have the money, summer camp and boarding school will be worth their weight in gold. Again, I would employ appeasement in explaining your reasoning to the child. They are special, they are destined for great things, it would be remiss of you to not give them every opportunity, they need to do this if they want to attain their potential for greatness in the world. You will miss them so much, and wish you could just be with them forever, it's so hard on you, etc, etc.

Other options would be getting him enrolled in after school programs, finding weekend activities to keep him occupied, or even buying him a dirt bike or moped so he can travel around, and get away from the house. Video games are also an option, especially since most video games today are designed for maximum addictiveness. In doing this, I would try to set up the room farthest away in the house, and most inaccessible, as the video game room (or build a tree-house). A distant basement room, or a playhouse outside, set up as a gaming room, and outfitted with a mini-fridge for sodas and snacks could keep him occupied indefinitely.

If you have other children, I would instead give each their own video game system, in their room, to keep them apart from each other. As a parent, one of your primary responsibilities should be to shield your other children from the narcissist, to protect them from ending up trembling wrecks, like Bob's brother, as adults. I would imagine there is little worse than having a narcissist older brother, stimulating your amygdala, and constantly deriving pleasure from the misery they fill every moment of your childhood with. (I suspect Bob's brother may have been the main guinea pig on whom Bob developed his amygdala hijacking skills.)

The primary goal is to put the narcissist in their own world, minimize interactions with them, and understand the limitations of your situation. You will not raise a stellar human being that you can be proud of. Thinking that you can change their personality disorder when you can't will only make you feel stressed and angry. Interacting with them will do little but give them practice in ruining your life. If you wish to be thorough, and have the funding, feel free to enroll them in therapy, but also understand that it will probably fail, and that it won't be your fault. You will fight the bravest battle, and do the best you can, but this isn't something you are likely to have any effect on. Just giving yourself and the rest of your family some measure of freedom and happiness, and creating a nice spot in a world which contains a narcissist, will be an enormous victory.

Finally, when they reach adulthood, understand that merely by enduring their noxiousness, you will have not only settled any debt you owed them, you will have left them perpetually in your debt. They will never repay you, of course, but in keeping that in mind, I hope you will realize that you have paid enough, and earned your freedom. Take a vacation, marvel at how nice the world is without that roiling vortex of angst, turmoil, and hatred in it, and then get as far away as you can. Grasp that every emotion is a manipulation, every entreaty a trap, and never look back.

Fellow Employees and Bosses

Sometimes you will have a coworker or boss who is a narcissist, and you will not want to leave your job. I do not have explicit experience with this, however the best advice I have seen came from this website,[1] where the individual described how he managed a boss with Narcissistic Personality Disorder.[2]

Basically, he and his coworkers found little jobs to give the narcissist to get him out of their hair, and keep him away from them. Narcissists tend to sabotage stuff, as in the case described on that site, so if the job you give the narcissist is important in any way, have somebody else perform a backup plan, so when the narcissist screws his job up, you can substitute the backup plan as needed. I would try to not let the narcissist know you are doing this. Just substitute the back-up plan when necessary, and act as if the narcissist contributed something useful.

---

[1]   "Memorable SOBs in Action" <http://mandynamerica.com/blog/memorable-sobs-in-inaction/> (Accessed 20 May 2014)

[2]   "Hendry, Plant Manager" <http://mandynamerica.com/blog/2011/06/03/190/> (Accessed 20 May 2014)

It is important to grasp that the amygdala does not just freak people out, but it also determines what specific item you focus on. Focusing a narcissist away from you, and on to something else can be enormously useful, and keep them occupied during the time they would otherwise spend making you miserable. Whether it is putting a narcissist child onto a video-game system, or getting a noxious coworker to drive over to the plant on the other side of town to do some busy work, success in the battle with the narcissist is sometimes not crushing them, but rather merely freeing yourself from their presence by focusing them elsewhere. Be creative.

It is also worth noting that narcissists sometimes will latch onto a person as a sort of "North Star," for guiding their own beliefs and perceptions. I don't know if this can be used in a work environment, but if it could, I suspect that you would have to be someone with whom the narcissist has limited contact.

In my experience, North Stars are usually people who have the respect of everyone, or who have the image of having the respect of everyone. It appears to me that this perception of universal respect permeates the narcissist's psyche, to the point that the narcissist will experience aversive stimulus when contemplating ideas which differ from that of their North Star, since they will worry that their ideas are wrong, or will be seen as wrong by the group, due to the North Star's influence.

Deep down, narcissists seem to know that something about their cognition is off, and prone to trip them up. I suspect that they have learned this after several times of losing their stature due to their malady. As a result, they sometimes will look around them, to see who everyone always agrees with. When they find a person whose conclusions are universally respected, they will reflexively adopt that person's positions, and often seek their approval. In the course of this, that person will assume an almost mythic reputation with the narcissist for always knowing what they are talking about, and always being right.

I imagine the narcissist has an even deeper linkage with that person than we will know, perhaps even fantasizing about being them, and thus cognitively mixing their own false reality of their own perfection with that person's perfection, and then reflecting that person's false perfection back upon themselves, since they are always in agreement with them (*"He and I have the same ideas, so we are equals in stature."*). It may even be amygdala assuaging to an insecure narcissist to tell themselves that they could never be out-grouped, because this un-out-group-able guru, and they, hold all the same positions and thoughts, and are practically the same person.

I've seen this a few times, but the one universal is that the narcissist will never seem to chose a close contact from their immediate social circle to turn into a North Star – it is almost always someone with whom they have very limited contact. This is probably related to the narcissist's need to feel in control of their immediate environment, their innate tendency to feel hostility and contempt for regular contacts, and their need to view themselves as the kings of their immediate fiefdom. I am fairly certain if you are a close contact with a narcissist you can never attain North Star status with them. But it might help someone who sees a narcissist at work, from a distance, to try and cultivate an image with the narcissist of being universally respected and admired by others, with an eye to keeping that distant narcissist under some form of control.

Marriage

Marriage to a narcissist is a little trickier. I would always advise divorce, to create a fully clean break, however in some circumstances, separation can work too. In conjunction with divorce or separation should be a physical separation of at least a few hundred miles. Getting away from a narcissist isn't the same if you are just going to keep bumping into them. To really quiet your mind, relax your amygdala, and reset things to the beginning, you need to know, on a very deep, fundamental level, that you will never see them again. This may sound extreme, but I would urge you to try it before you knock it. The effects of distance are indescribable.

There is the additional consideration that if you live nearby, the narcissist will almost certainly not go their own way in peace. Rather, they will harbor a grievance against you, it will prey upon their amygdala, and they will end up violating your space, and trying to perpetuate the relationship through acts ranging from bumping into you to start an argument, to committing acts of midnight vandalism at your house. The idea, of you, out there happy and free is among the most potent of amygdala stimulants, and they will feel that they will have to do something to assuage it, and release the pressure.

As a temporary salve, should divorce or separation prove unattainable in the short term, you can try to find work that involves travel, to get yourself out of the house. Most older people with job experience don't want to travel, so this is often a more available option than you would think. Also, you could join with some group or organization which requires your presence, but whose meetings the narcissist wouldn't want to attend.

The problem is that life is precious, and time is precious. There are good people out there, with whom you can join in some mutual pursuit, where you will all work together happily to attain a goal that you all want. If you are normal, that is what you are designed to do, and wasting time getting on that path is highly unsatisfying. Simply buying yourself a few moments of temporary freedom will not be the same, knowing that your real destiny, the real rebirth of your life, is being held in limbo by your screwed up circumstances in being tied to the narcissist. Always go for the clean break if you can.

However, this is war, and no one plan will suit every circumstance. If, for whatever reason, you feel it advantageous to buy time, and simply create some temporary distance, do so. But always try to keep your eye on making a clean break in the future. As an example, you might want to set up an anonymous legal entity with a lawyer, in one of the places you travel to, open a bank account for it, and begin depositing cash in it on your trips, for use as a freedom fund someday.

The key to buying time is appeasement. Narcissists do not want to think that you are abandoning them, nor do they want to feel like the type of inferior person someone would want to leave, nor do they want to picture you going off happy, while they are trapped in the hellhole of their own life and misery. Have no compunction about lying to them to assuage their amygdala's panic function – it is probably as kind to them as it is to you. Emphasize how unhappy you are at having to take that traveling job, emphasize how miserable it makes you, tell them how great they are, how jealous of them you are, since they don't have to leave, and so on, and so on. Then put them out of your mind as you sip a Mojito poolside at the resort you have to stay at, while on your travels.

In-laws

I receive a fair amount of email from people who are stuck with narcissist in-laws. This is probably the most tricky of relationships, because they might be able to create a rift with your spouse. If you and your spouse have children, it can be as if they hold the power of life or death over you. If your spouse doesn't understand what they are, and is acclimated to the noxiousness through a lifetime spent under their narcissist parent, it can also make escape nearly impossible.

So you are trapped. The first thing you need to do is assess how bad the narcissist is. How rule-governed is their behavior? Could they get so panicked at the thought of "losing" to you, that they will plant a bottle of poison in your house during a visit, poison themselves mildly, and then go to the ER so police will investigate and you will get blamed? Hopefully not, but if so, then you need to go the full documentary route described later on, complete with appeasing your spouse with stories of rising neighborhood crime rates, to explain your new found obsession with surveillance systems.

If they seem more rule governed, then I would try for appeasement during brief encounters, combined with minimizing interactions (and using more appeasement to explain the minimized interactions). You basically want to avoid the fight, and avoid having the narcissist focus that defective amygdala on you. Most really bad narcissists need somebody to use as an abuse sponge. By passively denying them the use of you in that regard, you make it very likely that they will focus their anger on someone else in their social/family circle. The more they focus that noxiousness on others, the easier it will be for you to out-group them with your spouse, should you ever end up the main target of their angst.

The other thing worth consideration, is that the narcissist is aging, and they will be worse, and thus easier to out-group, as time goes on. The narcissist is like a spy, maintaining the cover identity of a normal person that they can barely imagine being. Done simply for a month, as an undercover law-enforcement officer, that would be exhausting mentally. Every emotion you have, every action you take, you first have to think about, and calculate using the calculus of how someone else would act. Invariably, you will make a mistake, and when you do, you will experience the panic of potential exposure, and then replay the mistake in your head over and over, reliving it again and again, amping up your ambient stress levels ever higher.

For the narcissist, that is all they do, all the time, for their entire life. It is one thing, when you are twenty, and your brain is overflowing with cognitive capacity and brain power. But as the narcissist ages, neurons die back and their brain actually shrinks, like everyone else's. Their brain power diminishes, and they will grow ever less able to hide their malady. As this occurs, they are also forced to watch as their bodies begin to deteriorate, their youthful good looks sink below a sea of wrinkles and angry ugliness, and their options and opportunities in life dwindle.

Just as the narcissist's brain is losing the ability to hide what they are, all the stresses that produce their malady grow exponentially worse. They accidentally expose themselves with nonsensical rages, and then panic about having been found out. They accidentally reveal details about their life story that they realize they should have kept hidden. They alienate everyone, create alliances against themselves while in weakened positions, and then they curse their failures at strategic thinking. All of that stress only further weakens their mind and further erodes an already failing system.

If you can hold back the tide, if you can keep your fight with them at bay, an aging narcissist will prove to be their own worst enemy. It is like the old Sun Tzu adage, that if you sit by the river long enough, the bodies of your enemies will float by. Hold off your battle with the narcissist long enough, and they will destroy themselves with everyone around them, and you can sip your drink peacefully as the bloated, stinking body of their personality floats by you, and right out of your life.

If you are at war, your first goal should be to deny that there is a war. Make sure all aggression is directed against you, and that it is clearly explainable as acts of malice by your in-law. Emphasize to your spouse you aren't doing anything, and do not want to fight. If she want's the relationship between you and your in-laws amicable, she must understand that she will need to modify their behavior, not your's. You have done everything you can.

The problem you have is that normal people define themselves and their enemies by a deeper sense of right and wrong. The narcissist, however, defines their very essence by how the group views them, and how the group views their enemies. They are driven by a panicked need to see the group fortify their false reality, where they are good and you are evil. As a result, you will act with morals, and assume the group will not expel you because of your morality. However the narcissist acts under panic, solely to manipulate the opinion of the group, without any deeper sense of right and wrong. As a result, they have a whole plethora of tools at their disposal which you wouldn't even consider using, from outright lying, to criminal acts, and they are driven to use them by panic.

As a result, if you engage, you will likely be fighting a war, under a massive handicap, for a benefit that is likely minimal at best. Under normal stakes, this would be irritating enough. However if you add a marriage and children into the mix, the stakes can be astronomical, and the gain of victory minimal. The determination of your course will have to be made by you, based upon an understanding of the strength of your marital relationship, the nature of your spouse's relationship with their narcissist parents, and any other unique variables you see.

I can only advise you that your enemy, the narcissist, will almost always seek to out-group you within the family, and maybe within your marriage, using any and all nefarious and underhanded techniques, and that will give them any advantage. When that information is combined with the knowledge that the narcissist will only see their manipulative abilities, and their position within the group, deteriorate with time, often just executing a Fabian strategy of waiting them out may prove the best strategy of all.

Parents

I do not get many emails from the children of narcissists, presumably because recognizing the narcissist requires a certain degree of age and experience, and by the time people spot them, they are already set up to eject them from their lives. For that reason, this book won't have much advice in regard to dealing with narcissistic parents – there the only answer is to eject them from your lives. They will be just as miserable without you, as they were with you, no matter what they say, so don't feel bad about it.

It is possible that some other factor, like an inheritance, will crop up, leading you to want to preserve the relationship, without experiencing the misery. My opinion is, you can never maintain a relationship with a narcissist, without the misery, so you will just have to calculate if the misery of trying to appease them is worth the inheritance. One factor to add to your calculus is that narcissists who are able to draw narcissistic supply from appeasing victims, may live longer. It is only anecdotal, but the long lived narcissists I see always seem to have relatives that they are sucking life-force from. Deny them that life force, and they may just rot away in their own hatred and bitterness, and turn up their toes sooner.

In the event you are living with and caring for a narcissistic parent or in-law, I recommend using appeasement to facilitate separation by feigning financial difficulties. Use the financial difficulties to justify a reorganization of your life which removes the narcissist from it by necessity. Avoid any open acknowledgment of your understanding of what they are, their condition motivating the reorganization, or of the happiness you will experience once it is all over. As far as they are concerned, your life is hell, you are losing everything, and you dread the future you face.

Sell your house to consolidate your finances, move for a month or two to a furnished room in a less expensive area as far away as possible, and then complain about how in the gutter your life is. Seeing this, a narcissist parent would gleefully revel in the coming upheaval, and gladly trudge off to live a better life on their own, happily. After enough time has passed and you have cut contact as fully as possible, reorganize your life as you wish.

It is tempting to do the eviction and court-order stuff, imaging Sheriff's Deputies frog marching them out, and throwing them in the gutter, with the admonition, *"And don't come back!,"* but it won't work like that. They will find every legal loophole, you'll get irritated endlessly for a year or more, and the narcissist will revel in being the center of attention in this new drama where they can drag you over the legal coals at every turn.

Chapter Twenty

What If I Have Already
Been Out-Grouped?_____

These things are best dealt with early, but undoubtedly some readers will have only found this work after being successfully out-grouped within their family by the narcissist. Once the narcissist has turned everyone against you, it will be difficult to turn things around. First, you must accept that the group is probably lost to you, at least until people figure out the narcissist, which they will eventually, but maybe not in time for you.

It is tempting to look to change the situation around, perhaps by finding that one key piece of information that will show everyone what the narcissist is. Doing the big reveal, in front of everyone, to the horror of the narcissist, would certainly be rewarding. However, that is probably unrealistic, since the narcissist is a professional deep cover operative. The first thing I would do, is to begin trying to modify your own thought processes. Begin with an understanding of your own amygdala.

We all have an amygdala. The narcissist's is damaged, and freaks out with little stimulation, resulting in them trying to shield it with fantasy, and the sight of everyone else worse off. When they out-group you, they will create a circumstance which will amp up your own amygdala. You know the feeling. You are irritated, bothered, and suddenly your interactions with the group they've alienated you from become unpleasant. While in that state, you are less than pleasant too, because you are irritated – it's only natural. That needs to be fixed, as best as it possibly can, before anything else.

The first key to amygdala reprogramming in this situation, is to have an in-group. The narcissist has out-grouped you with one group, but if those idiots are under the narcissist's spell, they were a loser group to begin with. Find a good group, and join it. Might sky-diving be fun for you? Join a club. There are organizations for runners, bikers, motorcyclists, martial artists, shooting, golfing, and anything else you like, from goldfish clubs to horticulture. You can always volunteer, at things ranging from animal shelters, to volunteer fire departments. I would recommend the fire-department, martial arts, or shooting, as those guys will tend to be loyal, group-centric, happy to share their discipline with you, and prone to enjoy some beers after a get-together. Plus what they do is fun, and practical.

Once you have a real group, demote the idiots from the other group to associates, even if they are family. Truth be told, they aren't that smart, so you don't want to tie your star too tightly to them anyway. Now when you meet with them, your amygdala will instantly take it's activity down a notch, and you can begin to have fun watching the idiots circle the emotional drain that is the narcissist. Once you are no longer irritable, and your amygdala is less stimulated, people will notice, and you can begin showing them your kinder, gentler, more likable side. You can begin to offer to help them where you can, be kind to the weak, help the old ladies across the street, and so on. Make it so everyone wonders why the narcissist doesn't like you.

I'd be content there, but if you want to stir up trouble, you know the narcissist's trigger points. Begin befriending everyone, being pleasant all the time, and then one day laud someone's amazing accomplishments, in front of the narcissist. Play up how lucky they are to have such a great life. Extol their virtues, and all the things that they have, that the narcissist doesn't. Hit all the buttons – insufficiency, envy, insecurity, etc. Then make yourself scarce. Some other time, when you want the opinion of an expert in the narcissist's field, ask another member of the group for their opinion, in front of the narcissist, and place great weight upon what they think. If the narcissist interjects, announce you like the other guy's opinion better, and joke about him being smarter. Say that it makes more sense, and then take his side in the argument.

A normal person will blush as you laud them, and others will think you are being nice, but to the narcissist, that person will become an amygdala irritant, and they will turn on them eventually. Done right, it is as if you are using a secret code word to press the narcissist's buttons without anybody else knowing. If the person the narcissist turns on is liked by the group, you can create the same irritating situation for the narcissist that they created for you – the narcissist can try to get the irritant thrown out and see the group turn on them, or spend time in a group which contains an individual whose very presence irritates their amygdala, and whom they can't stand.

Know also that narcissists love to be the providers of information – the central hubs to whom everyone turns to be told new information, and how to think about it. Find out something important to the group from someone to whom you don't owe loyalty, and reveal it to the group in front of the narcissist. Or you can tell it to someone else to whom you don't owe loyalty, who will reveal it to the group. This will work best if the narcissist is hearing it for the first time as well. Once the narcissist knows where the information first came from, they will make a note to screw that person over sometime in the future, and if someone else revealed it, they will probably be targeted by the narcissist at some point as well.

Every time you point the narcissist at someone, and pull their trigger, you create bad feelings for one more piece of the group in the narcissist, and you turn one more piece of the group against the narcissist. Since the narcissist's whole malady is produced by their hair-trigger amygdala, you see how easy it can be to move the ball with just a little understanding of that trigger. Add in a little practice at doing it, and you can create some real havoc.

Even if you don't set the narcissist on someone, and you just maintain weak ties with the group, eventually the narcissist will expose themselves to everyone. In my experience, everyone will notice that something is off, and save memories of all the stuff that didn't fit – but they won't share these with anyone. One day there will be a critical mass of bad feelings built up, somebody will hesitatingly question the sanity and motives of the narcissist to somebody else, suddenly everyone will compare their extensive notes, and that will be it for the narcissist in that group. It usually happens suddenly.

Until then, enjoy your new group, and accept that your old group was weak and stupid, and you are better off without them anyway, should things ever go that way. If they come around great, if not, you have a great group to enjoy, while your former group revels in the the subtle pleasures of the narcissistic psychology.

Chapter Twenty-One

Case Studies of Extreme Scenarios_____

These are some situations which I have seen arise, or heard of arising, as a result of people having to deal with extreme narcissists. Minor details, unrelated to the salient point, may be changed, to protect the guilty, and the innocent. These stories are included here to help you see trouble coming, before it arrives. In my experience the bad narcissists are remarkably standardized in their psychology. As that amygdala becomes epically sensitive to freakouts, they seem to all begin to do the exact same behaviors over and over again, to try and quiet it. If your narcissist was bad enough to bring you to this book, they will likely be carbon copies of the characters in the following stories. Whether their threat ever rises to the level of those that follow will be more a matter of circumstances than their innate nature.

The Funeral

A widowed family Patriarch was dying, and a narcissist relative came in from out of town to stay in his house. His children didn't object, because being decent, they didn't want to be impolite during such a trying time. The relative proceeded to have a will drawn up by a lawyer friend that was designed to have all of the dying relative's belongings and property willed to them, specifically, on the basis that they could then apportion everything fairly. The relative then tried to get the Patriarch to sign it during a moment alone with him, while the Patriarch was in the hospital dying. The Patriarch acted confused, and refused to sign it. When questioned about it, the relative stated how important it was that the Patriarch's affairs be put in order, and stated they were just trying to help, since nobody was concerned about the legal aspects of his passing.

One relative had noted that the Patriarch had saved several thousand dollars in cash in a bed stand next to his bed at home. The money was left in the bed stand, out of respect to the parent (whom they hoped would recover and return home), and a desire by the child to not want to get involved with money issues in the family during the time of crisis. After the parent passed, most of the money was found missing. The narcissist denied taking it, but knowing all of the people involved, it was clearly the narcissist.

You will be imbued with a certain decency which will prevent you from doing things, that in protecting yourself and others you love, might be seen as rude or untrusting, by innocent parties. When dealing with the narcissist, understand that they have the exact opposite urges you have. If there is money on the table, you need to take it, and keep it safe. Appease the narcissist, by saying you don't want a burglar to take it, but secure it first, at all costs. Don't give them opportunities to screw you and your loved ones, such as by leaving them alone with a dying relative who is delirious, and who might sign papers that are explicitly designed to screw you, or by leaving the narcissist with any cash or valuables that they could steal. Secure everything of value, from papers to mementos, to money and property.

The money taken was the beginning of the fraying of the familial bonds with this narcissist. By the time the Patriarch's funeral had arrived, nobody could physically tolerate the presence of the narcissist due to their noxiousness, so they were left alone in the Patriarch's house. The narcissist ordered a moving van, and cleared as much of the Patriarch's possessions as possible out, into the van, and split.

This was unfortunate as it included all of the family photos, and numerous keepsakes and mementos that the rest of the family would like to have seen preserved. Again, my own suspicion is that all of that was taken specifically to produce unhappiness in the rest of the family.

It worked out in the end however, as one child had acquired the services of an excellent estate lawyer, who promptly billed all of the taken material to that relative's portion of the estate, thereby allowing the remaining relatives to at least acquire financial recompense for the lost items. I am sure, knowing the parties involved, that the narcissist was infuriated to see the denial of an amount from the will which would probably have surpassed, by some measure, the real value of what they took. Although they threatened to sue, the costs involved proved prohibitive, and the matter was dropped.

Deeds and Trusts

I knew two married lawyers, one of whom, the man, was a raging narcissist. He had actually placed all of their family property into some sort of trust, of which he was the sole trustee. He had justified this under some legal reasoning which involved reduced tax burdens, but I assume this afforded him some increased level of sole control over all of the familial assets. His wife trusted him, and never thought twice about it. To increase his level of control even more, he apparently secured all the signed trusts and related deeds and documents in his office, but never filed them officially.

Once trouble began, his wife, being smart, managed to secure all the copies of the trusts and deeds without his knowledge. He subsequently got terminally ill, and with all the increased rage and abuse, she decided to clear out, but not divorce him, given the proximity of his end. When he went to look for the signed trusts and deeds, to dispose of the family assets as he wanted, they were all gone. He died before he could divorce her, and she ended up with all the family assets.

The key to dealing with a narcissist successfully, in such an environment, is to realize early that you have a problem with them, realize the full magnitude of it, and take any and all actions you can to protect yourself later on, as soon as possible. The narcissist realizes that there is a problem long before you do (in truth, they hate everyone, so they always view you as an enemy), but they will be hesitant to act decisively on their perceptions, for fear of alerting you to the problems that they see. They try to be, above all else, the snake in the grass. This will often give you a brief window to act, before open hostilities emerge.

Also, they tend to focus more on the immediate need to inflict harm *at that moment*, rather than planning carefully to be able to inflict maximum pain in the future. Even as hostilities break out, the narcissist will often not realize that they are true hostilities, merely viewing them as normal SNAFUs that will blow over.

Here, the narcissist, very early on, while his wife still thought him loyal, was trying to secure his sole control over familial assets, so if hostilities broke out, he could screw over his wife completely. I assume, had he found the papers, he would have sold off all of the family assets, and given the money to a charity right before he died, or sought to use his control over them to traumatize his wife some other way. Had his wife not realized in the nick of time that there was a problem, and gotten those papers, her financial situation would have been much worse.

You need to be honest with yourself, acknowledge there is a problem early, and begin looking forward to how the narcissist might try to screw you and your family. If there is money in a joint bank account, the narcissist will drain it and lose it. If there is any sort of loan which can be drawn down to increase debt, the narcissist will do that. If there are credit card bills that can be run up, assume they will do that. Recognize that the narcissist will cut off their own arm with a chainsaw, if they can take your pinky finger with it. They are a unique psychology, in that they are often selflessly evil – all that matters to them is your suffering, and they will endure immense hardships happily, to bring it about.

So once war breaks out, they will seek to stimulate your amygdala however they can. If you have left open some vulnerability, by which the narcissist can freak you out, they will use it. You need to examine your situation, assess every possible vulnerability (in the context of an enemy who will take themselves down with you, if necessary), and take any measure you can to reduce your exposure to being screwed over, *in advance of the full hostilities beginning*. The key is to assess every vulnerability, and then neutralize all of them, all at once, before the narcissist realizes what you have done.

Secure your legal papers, empty joint bank accounts, drain any available loan, secure any cash, cancel any credit cards, and try to think of how you would attack yourself, if you were a soulless psychopath bent on evil, and happily willing to hurt yourself to hurt others. Then protect yourself as unobtrusively and surreptitiously as possible. If possible, the narcissist should have no idea that you have protected yourself, and if they do find out, you should try to have an innocuous reason for what you did, such as a faked fear of the threat of identity theft, or a desire to simplify the paperwork in your life.

You Need a Team

You need a team to deal with the narcissist. If they have isolated you, you need to find an online forum, and talk with people about what is going on. Rehashing experiences can be enormously useful. While you are in the clutches of the narcissist, your amygdala is in high gear, to the point of overload. Under such conditions, your amygdala will have a diminished ability to read the environment, connect dots, predict the future, and contextualize the past. Without a relaxed amygdala, we are all blind to the world.

As an example, a narcissist was driving with his wife's sister. He began talking about how badly he was begin treated by his wife, and offhandedly said, "*She doesn't tell me anything any more. I mean, we all hope she lives a long time, but suppose something happened to her. I wouldn't even know where to collect her life insurance.*" He then immediately looked intently at the sister, as if waiting for a specific response. She offhandedly said, "*I assume you'd figure it out.*" She then returned to looking out the window, and not talking with the narcissist, to avoid his noxiousness.

She later returned home, and only recounted the conversation after being asked by her husband what the narcissist had talked about. No sooner had the words left her mouth, than she realized the narcissist was, in reality, fishing around to try and find out where to go to collect his wife's life insurance, or check on the policy status. She immediately called and told her sister who took protective measures, and probably averted her own horrific end.

The problem is, people who are exposed to a narcissist learn to tune them out. Whenever your amygdala contacts them, it is revulsed, so it actually learns to actively drive your focus away from them without your conscious knowledge, to protect your brain from the awfulness. I know one guy whose brain shuts down around his narcissist, rendering him almost totally unable to think or function.

If the narcissist talks, your brain will start you daydreaming about something else, and you will not hear what they say, let alone wonder why they are saying it. If you try to think about something they did, your amygdala will shift your focus to something nice, and you will miss the motives behind it. In the end, you need someone to talk to for many reasons - to get fresh eyes on your problem, to rehash the important points, to see the things you are missing because your brain is too exhausted, and to help you keep your grip on sanity, as you wrestle with a personality that is so bad, no normal person could believe that it is real.

Find someone you can trust, or several people you can trust, and keep them in the loop on your problems. Talk events over with them. If need be, hire a psychological professional to run things by. But don't try to fight the battle alone.

The Vandal

One narcissist, after splitting with her spouse, made repeated nighttime visits to the spouse's home, to vandalize his car. Again, this was amygdala hyperactivity. In her head, the thought of her husband having won, and gotten rid of her, so irritated her that she had to return to his house, and vandalize his car, to assuage the anxiety and frustration produced by imagining him happy. One of the visits resulted in her breaking something in such a way that when he went to use it, he would have been injured or killed. It was discovered by sheer luck before anyone was hurt.

This story is included to remind you that getting free of your narcissist is not necessarily the end of your story. You will want to be aware, that a damaged psychology, prone to epically freak out over your happiness, may not just go away after you break free of it and find happiness without them.

You should assume, if you live in close proximity to your narcissist that they will be back, and violate your personal space. Take measures, such as security cameras and motion detectors, to protect yourself and your property from harm. Bear in mind, nothing is as valuable in a court of law as video of a psycho lurking outside your house at 2 AM in the morning, doing vandalism to your belongings. And nothing will trigger a narcissist's amygdala more than you letting them know that you have irrefutable video evidence of them grossly transgressing the boundaries of right and wrong, as well as the law.

In this case the vandal was eventually caught on video plying her trade, and the video was used to essentially force the narcissist to abandon the relative fully, under threat of future prosecution and public exposure.

The Monster

In another famous case, a very pretty girl who broke free of her narcissist received a call from him on her cell phone. He said he wanted to give her a gift, as a way of apologizing for how he had treated her. She agreed to go outside her house to receive the gift, if he would acknowledge that their relationship was over, and then leave her alone. He did, and she went outside. There, a friend of the narcissist who was waiting, walked up and threw acid in her face, disfiguring her for life. The narcissist and his friend ended up in prison, but the damage was done.

Never underestimate these characters. There is a story of a rocket scientist who poisoned the husband of a woman he had a crush on in high school. The story begins with how decades after he knew the woman, he broke into her house, and poisoned a drink in the refrigerator. He used a reagent designed to give the husband cancer, but he overdosed it, and as a result the symptoms presented acutely, and drew the attention of authorities. The poisoned drink killed her husband and a 10 year old niece. A book on the case subsequently alleged that the wife had actually been the instigator, and the whole thing was a plot to get rid of her husband, using her old flame to do the dirty work. The very nature of the allegation, combined with your knowledge of the mind-bending reality that surrounds narcissists, should give you an idea of just how paranoid you should be.

The problem is that narcissists are driven by sheer panic, and a fear of an emotional imbalance so severe, that they can't think logically – everything is at the whim of wholly illogical emotions. As a result, you can't predict accurately what they are capable of, using your thought patterns and logical reasoning as a metric. If your narcissist is so bad that you have sought out a book like this, and your relationship progresses to the point that you have no choice but to break contact, just keep an ear open for that little voice in the back of your head that warns you of danger, and don't be afraid to be paranoid. With narcissists, sometimes they really are out to get you.

Chapter Twenty-Two

Never Let the Narcissist Win

If you need the advice in this section, you have ended up in a war with your narcissist. First, the most basic rule should be, never allow the narcissist a victory. Narcissists are wracked with insecurity and perceptions of inferiority. Their entire life is defined by the misery of feeling that they are the loser, and desperately trying to find any rationale for denying this to themselves. If every interaction with you is a loss, then the narcissist will quickly come to attach the thought of encountering you, with the feelings of despair, defeat, and inferiority that they dread so much. Pretty soon, they will avoid interacting with you, since each interaction and defeat will only prove more depressing.

But if they can attain even a single victory, that victory can give them relief from the agony of their pathetic lives. Suddenly they can tell themselves that they aren't a loser, because they beat you. It is a tangible, real reinforcement of their false reality. To the narcissist, that ability to deny their own insecurity with some tangible fact is like a heroin high. The danger is that they will become addicted, and begin returning for more. You want them beat down, dejected, and demoralized every time they think of dealing with you, not energized, uplifted, and eager to find another way to screw you over.

There is a legal strategy which basically entails dragging someone through court, in a case which is unlikely to be won, merely to force the other individual to incur legal costs and loss of time. A normal individual will accurately calculate that the costs and time lost may render such a fight costly and painful. However, if the narcissist successfully defends against such a case, they will experience a drug-like high, produced by seeing an official body such as a court, officially judge you to be an "*evil loser*," and them to be a "*noble and righteous winner."* If that occurs, not only won't they be chastened at the thought of engaging you in the future, they may actually want more such encounters, to feed their false reality of themselves as noble, and you as evil.

For that reason, you must never allow the narcissist a win. Even if you judge something important, do not go to war over it if you feel you will lose to the narcissist. Throw it away, and define your battlefield elsewhere. Nothing tangible is worth having to deal with a narcissist regularly.

In defining your battlefield elsewhere, and judging the issue the narcissist would win on as unimportant to you, you exploit another quirk of the narcissist's mind. Narcissist don't have a clear grasp on truth. Perhaps because their brain is so accustomed to bending reality to assuage their insecurity, they will often define reality by gauging and mirroring the perceptions of others.

Thus, a narcissist, enduring a minor defeat of minimal importance, can find themselves horrified if everyone else judges the loss decisive, and defining. Let a narcissist see everyone laugh at them, and taunt them over a minor loss, and they might as well have lost everything – it will be crushing to them. Conversely, I have noticed that even a substantial victory, treated as wholly unimportant by others, and ignored by everyone, can leave the narcissist dejected and demoralized. Their expression will almost bemoan that they spent so much time and effort, pursuing a victory which wasn't even important. (Perhaps ACC error-monitoring activation, produced by a violation of expectation, adds to this effect.)

Part of it may also relate to the fact that the narcissist needs you miserable, on a very deep, psychological level. Much of interpersonal narcissist psychology can be best understood by viewing them as individuals whose brains are stuck in *"revenge mode,"* in such a way that they reflexively want revenge on everyone they meet, whether that person has transgressed against them or not. That single urge, will almost define their interpersonal interactions. As a result, their ideal victory is not defined by scale or nature, but by the horror you experience in response to it. Give a narcissist the most minor victory, but let you be horrified by it, and rendered a trembling wreck, and the narcissist will rejoice. Let them acquire the most hard-earned, substantial victory, but you not care (or worse, go off happy, as if nothing happened), and they will be crushed.

Because of all of this, the first rule you should have in warring with your narcissist, should be to never allow them a single victory. Use your ability to pick your battles, and define your battlefield to deny them any positive outcome when engaging with you. If they do win, act as if you never cared to begin with, and are puzzled why it was so important to them. Even imply, in a carefree, amused manner, that they are weird for caring so much. Fail to do this, and your narcissist will come back.

Chapter Twenty-Three

Document Everything _____

If you enter a war with the narcissist, and any aspect of it might end up in court, you should understand that documentary proof is invaluable. If things go to court, the narcissist's goal is to present their false reality to the court, and get the court to believe it. All too often, this becomes a contest between your perception of reality, and the narcissist's, and maybe you win, maybe you don't. That is unacceptable, especially since you should be focusing on making every encounter with you a loss for the narcissist.

The narcissist lives in a false reality of made up perceptions designed to make them look righteous and noble. In a very real way, they are cognitively allergic to reality. Having an inarguable, legal record of reality, and presenting it to the narcissist in an official public forum like a court, is like force feeding them gobs of the reality they are so highly allergic to. Of course, in my experience, such a record can be worth even more out of court, both to facilitate future amygdala hijacks, and to secure your own personal safety.

Your first order of business is to keep a daily journal, with each entry dated and signed. Write down everything of note which happens to you, any potential means of corroboration, and the event's significance to you. In court, a written record, created contemporaneously with events, is given much greater weight than a witness' testimony, delivered months later, and subject to distortions with time.

If your narcissist testifies "X," and you can show that at the time, you wrote "Y" in a signed and dated entry in your journal, this will have two effects. First it proves your case to the court. Second it executes a major amygdala hijack on your narcissist which will demoralize him, demotivate him, and reduce his cognitive ability. The court will take your side, and treat his testimony as worthless and unimportant by comparison.

Your second order of business should be to funnel as much communication as you can through email, written letters (keep photocopies of all of yours, that you sent) and text messages. If it is legal to do so in your state, you should also record any phone conversations as well. Again, your narcissist's goal is to create a false reality which portrays him as noble and righteous. Nothing will freak him out as much as placing his false reality before the court, and then seeing you introduce documentary evidence which shows him to be a mentally unbalanced liar. Such evidence not only tears his entire case to shreds – it proves to the court that his false reality, where he is noble and righteous, is complete baloney, and it replaces that false reality with a factual finding of his moral degeneracy - placed in the official court record.

If you have the funds, there are recording devices which are designed to look like buttons, sunglasses, or some other innocent clothing item. They will record video and sound to a small hard-drive the size of a pack of cigarettes, which also contains the rechargeable power supply. Cell phones today all have voice recorders. Take to carrying items like this with you, to document any interactions you have with the narcissist.

Set up video surveillance around your house, and even in it. You can buy night vision security cameras and the cables and video recorder for them, for a few hundred dollars at box store, and online you can easily find cameras made to look like clocks and Teddy Bears for inside your house. Keep them running while you are gone, set to record only if motion-triggered, and keep an eye on whether the narcissist is entering your home, or on your property. If you get back, and there are no videos recorded, you know your home was secure. If there are videos, you will have excellent evidence of your narcissist's boundary transgressions, for use in court, or to out-group them with family and friends, on the grounds of them being untrustworthy nut-jobs.

Such evidence, known to the narcissist to be under your control, can be like holding the power of life or death over the narcissist, and can allow you to acquire substantial leverage against them in the future. You will literally have, in your hands, the power to shred their false reality, and construct a new one with them as tangibly evil. They will do anything to keep everyone else from seeing their real nature, and the depth of their illness, because deep inside, they fear nothing as much as everyone beginning to question their sanity and motives. They know that single thread, presented to everyone, could unravel every falsehood supporting the myth of their life.

Do note that such recording can be a tricky legal area however, with laws that vary according to jurisdiction. Be sure when you record your narcissist, that you are in compliance with all laws for your federal, state, and local jurisdictions. If it is in your house, or on your property, you will almost always be allowed to do as you please, but do consult with a lawyer. Don't break any laws here, or step over the line by hacking their email account, or illegally accessing their voice mail, or recording a private conversation in a jurisdiction which does not allow that without all parties being aware of the recording. Nor should you openly blackmail your narcissist in a way that you wouldn't want law enforcement made aware of. Narcissists will love nothing more than to use rules against you. Don't give them the satisfaction.

From there, you want to try and keep as many records as possible, to document your narcissist's evil ways. Hate filled letters, angry voice mails, and any police reports about vandalism or other transgressions should all be saved - and noted in your journal.

Finally, narcissists are prone to freak out over anyone recording them. Although I don't advise that you should purposely provoke your narcissist, you should be aware that making a point of openly videotaping them whenever they are around you, "for your safety," can sometimes trigger an amygdala hijack all by itself. The result of such a strategy is to either force civil behavior out of a narcissist who would otherwise be anything but civil, or produce a video of a raving loon which will play wonderfully in court. Either way, you will win.

Chapter Twenty-Four

Visualizing the Narcissist's World _____

One of the things which has haunted me is how stupid the narcissists I have known were, yet how complex their emotional manipulations were, and how deep their grasp of the workings of the mind have been. One of the first things which held me back in understanding them was the fact that I could not believe that such rank idiots could have such a nuanced and subtle understanding of complex cognition.

They knew things innately that I only figured out after a long period spent in extensive study and deep contemplation. My schooling, the things I studied and excelled at, and my mental abilities, far exceeded anything they could have ever dreamed of accomplishing. Yet, they understood and played each person around them like a Stradivarius, as I struggled to even figure out how these rank idiots would see the world, or how they might be able to be manipulated. How could such idiots have known so much? It was baffling, but I suspect the following is the answer, or at least a significant part of it.

Imagine that your amygdala can only focus on one thing. (This is actually not far from the truth. Try following two conversations at once, and keeping yourself fully apprised of what is going on in both. Your amygdala will want to pick one, and you will probably find yourself focusing on one, and then flipping back to the other.) When you deal with people, especially in pursuit of some goal, there will often be two primary things competing for your attention. Here, using a conversation analogy, we will call them the two conversations.

The first conversation that your amygdala will focus on is the impersonal, or as I think of it, the technical. This is the facts, objectives, strictures, and other technical details relating to the purpose and objective of your interaction. Suppose I come to you, a normal person, and ask, *"How do we solve this problem?"* Your response will be to focus on the technical aspects of the problem. To the extent that you notice any emotion, it will probably be emotion related to the nature of the problem, such as, do I look panicked, indicating this problem is intimidating and difficult, or do I look enthused, indicating that solving this problem will lead to a big payoff, and it probably isn't that hard to solve. You are focused on the technical.

The second item competing for your attention is, how does this person talking to you feel? What are their facial affects, body postures, and other emotional indicators telling you about what is going on inside of them? This is a second "conversation" that you have the option of listening to, but if you are goal-oriented, you will probably ignore it, unless some aspect of it relates to the goal at hand. Dianne Sawyer frequently looks extraordinarily anguished around her eyebrows and cheeks when she reads the evening news, but nobody notices, because they are focused on the news. Supreme Court Justice John Roberts frequently has extraordinarily panicked/startled eyes, even when smiling, but nobody really comments on that, beyond an AP photographer who once sent a cropped picture of just his eyes out over the wire.

As I have learned to look at this second "conversation" in the people I meet, I frequently see sad downmouths, depressed eyebrows, happy eyes, angry brow ridges, angry eyes, defensively hunched shoulders, clipped/choppy muscle movement patterns, happy bouncing walks, and so forth. This second conversation, competing for your amygdala's attention, is actually quite rich in content, but most people disregard it. They never teach their amygdala to flag the relevant emotional expressions as significant, connect the relevant expressions to their relevant emotions, or learn to imagine how what their associate is *"feeling,"* might inform his thought processes, decisions, or actions. Even fewer still, take in this information, process it, and then calculate mentally how best to alter the emotions they see to create a world emotionally predisposed to serving their own interests. Most people focus on the task at hand, and ignore the emotional state of the people around them.

If you have adopted this technical cognitive model, you can accomplish great things. You can actually mold the world around you, physically, through your conscious, sentient manipulation of the physical material of which it is made. But there is another means of manipulation, and it is powerful too.

If you are reading this, you have likely found your physical world rendered much less enjoyable, and none of your technical abilities, or your technical cognitive model, could have any effect to ameliorate this. Even worse you have watched as an idiot who you would kill in a state of nature has effortlessly done all of this, and it has taken every fiber of your being to try to undo some of the damage.

Using the technical model to try and combat the narcissist is poor medicine in our rule and law-bound world, so if you have not learned to listen in on this second, emotional "conversation," you will have seen the power of that data in that conversation firsthand. You may be the business owner who hired a passive-aggressive narcissist - who promptly manufactured grievances in his head against everyone, and then set about evening the score with passive aggressive sabotage of your workplace, all while feigning normalcy. Maybe you just ended up married to a narcissist, and found your whole life torn asunder, despite your being so much smarter than them.

That all happened because you tried to be the technical, logical force, reasoning with an emotional idiot, whose entire cognitive model perceived only emotion, manipulated only emotion, and was even motivated solely by emotion.

In the end, that is what you should try to process about the narcissist. They only listen to that second, emotional "conversation." The first technical one, they can't hear. Maybe they are too stupid, maybe they are too lazy, maybe they don't care, or maybe, being solely motivated by emotion, they assume emotion is what motivates everyone else as well, and thus they see the technical as unimportant.

Once you begin to grasp this dichotomy in cognitive models, you begin to understand how the narcissist will not listen too closely to technical facts which are negative, in the view of their ego. You will understand how they can create a false-reality composed of wholly imaginary facts, and view reality itself as malleable. You will even see why they will do stupid things which will destroy their entire lives. They are actually disconnected from the technical reality of the world, beginning at the point where the technical conversation first enters a human's head.

We hold facts above all else, endure the emotions they produce, and then use those negative emotions to motivate us to try and tangibly alter our reality, to make the facts we perceive in it less negative. The narcissist holds emotion paramount, and everything is tailored to serve that. They will alter any facts they need to, in order to create positive emotions. They will allow any negative reality to overtake them, if altering that reality would require enduring negative emotions by listening to that first, technical conversation.

This divergence probably begins in childhood, with that first emotional short circuit, when the narcissist alters their perceptions, to deny a *"bad"* fact's existence and assuage a negative emotion. At that moment, such a nascent neural circuit created, offers such an easy means to assuage negative emotion, that it will rapidly become a go-to circuit to shut off bad emotion.

Conscious alteration of a reality is hard, painful work. To motivate it, you must endure bad emotions, suffer through hard trials and exhaustive efforts, and even then, you may sometimes fail. How much easier to retreat into the neural circuitry of your head, construct a false reality, and then see all those negative emotions vanish, as if by magic, and with no effort or pain whatsoever.

But the brain is like a muscle. It adapts to do what it does often – especially during those early developmental years when the brain is most plastic and adaptable. If you are routinely denying facts and holding emotion paramount in your mind, it would seem inevitable that you would eventually end up pursing a more emotional cognitive model. As your reality becomes worse and worse, it will drive you even deeper into your emotionally driven, reality-detached cognitive model.

Once you inhabit delusions, the idea of leaving them is too traumatic to contemplate. Once you cannot allow yourself to be forced from your delusion, you will confront that other people's perceptions are the primary threat to your delusions. The first thing the King with no clothes will notice is the person who tells him he's naked.

Once you realize that the intrusions of the perceptions of others is your primary threat, you are left with little choice but to try and find ways to trick everyone else into sharing those delusions, through the only form of manipulation you understand – the emotional. Once you focus on trying to manipulate others into delusion, it creates a character exactly like the one you knew. They are the people, that each normal person they encounter, will one day sit around stunned at, wondering how anyone ever bought into anything they said. The truth is, they were trained from childhood to make everyone emotionally buy into their delusion, and their early focus on the second, emotional conversation was a key part of their success.

As you begin to notice this dichotomy, you will see it everywhere. You will understand the narcissist who had everything, threw it away to hurt other people, and ends up dying alone and miserable - abused by staff in a nursing home without anyone to turn to. You will understand those in society who continue to advocate for spending their government into fiscal ruin, even as the impending ruin becomes not only logically obvious, but impossible to ignore. Cutting back would produce upset emotions in the nation, and nothing is as important as us all avoiding upset emotions. Even the alternative right defines a fundamental mover of the left as a fear of *"feel bad."* That is the second conversation, brought to the fore, and captured in a phrase. It is the sole mover of all of this, because it is all that these people's brains are designed to see.

When this emotion-based cognitive model strikes, it is very difficult to counter, if you do not pay attention to it, or listen to that second conversation yourself. The very fact that soon the United States, the greatest country in the history of the world will collapse economically, purely due to this cognitive model's prevalence, should highlight better than anything, the power of it. All of our logic and technical understanding, and we patriots are nearly helpless to avert the coming collapse – in large part because we do not partake of that second conversation, or the battle which grows from it. It should also highlight just how strange it is that so many people do not pay more attention to the second, emotional conversation, given its enormous power.

My advice is, once you are free of your narcissist, train yourself to listen to this second conversation. Make a study of the facial expressions of those around you. How do they stand - upright and interested, or hunched over and guarded? Are their movements slow and casual, bouncing and joyful, or fast and choppy? Are their shoulders

189

broad and relaxed, or pinched up and braced? Why are they that way? What are they feeling, and what they are telling you? What emotion underlies everything that they say and do? Your understanding of the narcissist will expand radically, but that will be nothing compared to your understanding of people.

Chapter Twenty-Five

Spotting the Narcissist _____

Oh, to be able to go back in time, and know who was a narcissist, before letting them into your life. I have distinct memories of early signs I saw that clearly indicated mental dysfunction, but which I assumed were limited to a very narrow incident, and of minimal importance. From bizarre freakouts, to denial of things I not only knew to be true, but which I knew the narcissist knew were true as well.

This brings us to the first rule of spotting the narcissist - namely that what you notice is almost certainly significant, if it was significant enough to be noticed in the first place. If you have noticed aberrant behavior, in an individual trying to appear normal, then you have noticed a sign that, although minimal on the outside, likely harbors much greater significance with respect to what is going on inside of them. You need to focus on what you saw, and understand just how important it is.

There are many different warning signs. Strained relationships with family are, of course, not dispositive, but can be indicative, especially if the family members are compassionate and likable. Lack of close relationships with friends from work or otherwise can also be indicative, as can a troubled work history.

Narcissists tend to not do so well when they need to stifle their noxious urges, to establish stable relationships with regular contacts, be it family or work. A constant work environment spent dealing with others will frequently break them, as sooner or later they will exhibit a rage, and they will assume that rage has outed them as crazy. Then their amygdala will enter high gear all the time in response to that stress. That will make hiding their malady harder to hide, that will make another rage more likely, and everything will go downhill from there.

This will often lead them to either seek out work which involves limited contact with others, or work in which the contact with others is confrontational (ie lawyering, politics, or a position of authority). Wherever the narcissist tries to establish stable relationships, they will only succeed as long as they can foster an illusion among those around them of normalcy. If they try to hold normal jobs, they will only last as long as they can maintain their normal facade, which is usually a short period of time. In the worst of narcissists, this will result in a long string of jobs, never quite leading to firing, but never quite leading to a rewarding career, or long-lasting friendships.

The one exception to the unsuccessful worker rule is the narcissist who derives amygdala relief from his work. A narcissist who assuages his amygdala at work can become quite motivated, and quite successful, or hold his job for a long time. The BTK (Bind Torture Kill) serial killer actually not only held his Code Enforcement job quite successfully, he so enjoyed tormenting people over petty legal issues such as the height of their lawn, that he abandoned serial killing – a rare event which led authorities to think he must have died or been imprisoned. Politicians, lawyers, other professional grievance agents, or simply positions of power which allow a narcissist to validate their delusions of grandeur, or to torment people, can all lead to a narcissist becoming quite "successful" in that particular role, if they can find their way into it. If someone defines their life and themselves by their job or position, rather than who they are and the loved ones around them, watch out.

I've also noticed some narcissists have stressful voices, designed to assert their dominance, and forestall any challenges to what they say. A booming voice, over-emphasis to the point of intimidation, or just subtle nuances of anger or irritation can all be indicative.

Another good detector can be aggressive dog breeds. Narcissists have a subtle stress response that many dogs seem to detect. Three dogs, one of them mine, attacked my narcissist Bob, in different incidents over several years - all seemingly for no perceptible reason. I foolishly ignored that. Take your potential narcissist shopping for Rottweiler puppies, and see how the adult Rotty parents interact with him. If they are nice to you, but he loses an arm, you may very well have a narcissist.

Of course you may be the best detector of narcissists yourself, already. If you have already dealt extensively enough with a narcissist to seek out a text on the subject, you will already have trained yourself to detect many of the subtle aspects of their psychology, whether you are aware of it or not. Meet a new narcissist, and you will begin to feel many of the negative sensations your old narcissist evoked. The real key is to learn to listen to that inner voice, and heed its warning. Similarly to how you disregarded warning signs with your main narcissist, you will be tempted to think that you are being paranoid, or hyper-sensitive with subsequent narcissists you meet.

The main thing I notice about narcissists is what I used to refer to as their high stress level, and fearful, amped personae. I used to think that they listened with a slight sense of panic or agitation. However I have seen others who had the look, but not as much of the fearful intensity, replacing it with a smoldering anger. Lately I am beginning to think that what I am seeing is not intensity, so much as expectancy. The Narcissist is waiting, expectantly, to see what they think should happen. Some wait in fear, some wait angry, some wait anguished, but they are all on guard, for the triggering stimulus which aggravates their condition. Perhaps their ACC is primed to release a neural alarm if things don't go as expected, so they are watching intently to make sure everything fits their expectations. Maybe they live a life filled with the false expectations of their false reality, and this makes them live each moment on guard for any piece of data which will violate expectations, and pierce their narcissistic bubble. Eventually the waiting is so conditioned, that it even permeates their expression.

This will also tend to manifest in some level of fear, anger, or sadness within their neutral facial expression. The brain's stress center, the amygdala, is wired to the facial muscles through the facial nerve. When experiencing stress, one need not consciously seek to wear a stressed facial expression. Rather, that will be taken care of without conscious thought, by the brain calling up the expression without conscious awareness. Because of this, many narcissists will commonly carry a subtle undercurrent of an expression that is angry, anguished, disgusted, overly intense, or fearful. Other situation-specific expressions will be laid over this, but they will tend to be infected by the underlying expression which reflects the narcissist's underlying base response to

193

stressors. This can seemingly make normal expression more difficult, and straining to the narcissist.

One narcissist looked at video of United States Senator Richard Lugar, and enthusiastically pointed out how perfect Lugar's face was, because it always carried the appearance of a smile, even at rest. As a result, he noted, Lugar's facial muscles never had to get tired when he smiled. The narcissist in question carried a very strong expression of pained sadness and anguish when his face was at rest – an affect which was still visible when he would try to fake a smile. Presumably the statement was an outgrowth of his pondering how much his own face hurt when he would try to smile.

That brings us to another narcissist indicator. If you are normal, many of the narcissist's insights would never occur to you. I have never noted my face being tired when I smile, because when I smile, I am focused on the happy thought making me smile. Not so, the narcissist. They will come out with puzzling things that you would never say, and which will briefly make you pause, to contemplate them.

As one example, narcissists operate with an innate perception that everyone is out to screw them, and they will often say things which indicate a view of an overly hostile world. They view the world as hostile, because they are hostile, and they can't imagine why anyone wouldn't be. Bob used to rail about what an idiot I was, because I didn't understand how everyone was out to screw me, and if I knew how things worked, I would be out to screw everyone else myself. In Bob's head, everyone was like him, so everyone was out to screw everyone else. I was a rare idiot, who didn't realize that was how the world worked, so when he wanted to reinforce his perception of my intellectual inferiority with a factual support, he would restate that I was oblivious to this clear truth.

Narcissists will also recognize other narcissists, and keep their distance from them. Other narcissists know how the world works, so they are dangerous compared to the idiots who still think a lot of people are good, and can be trusted.

Another sign I have noted is the need to diminish others, to build up themselves. Narcissists will constantly find fault with the people around them. I cannot remember one person whom Bob did not, at one time or other, make disparaging, demeaning comments about. Usually these comments will impugn a person's moral character, accomplishments, abilities, status, fortitude, or their appearance. They will be designed to imply that not only is the narcissist beyond reproach with respect to the cited quality – they are so elevated as to be the unquestioned arbiter of everyone else's abilities in that regard. I suspect the nature of the comments will tell you much about the narcissist, as each comment is designed to assuage the narcissist's own insecurity over the same issue. If non-narcissist Tom is of poor moral fiber, then narcissist Bob must be better morally by comparison. If non-narcissist John is incapable in some regard, then narcissist Bob must be an authority on it by comparison. Watch for someone trying to tell you how others are inferior, and ask yourself, how often do you make a point to tell one friend, how some other friend is inferior. If you are not insecure about your own attributes, you will never do it.

Another sign you can look for is drawing an unusual degree of pleasure from your exertions. A non-narcissist will tend to offer to pitch in when you try to help them, and feel uncomfortable when others exert themselves on their behalf. At the very least, exertions on their behalf should produce a strong appreciation. But not in the narcissist. Put yourself out, ridiculously for the narcissist, and not only won't they offer to pitch in, their eyes will glaze over with pleasure, they will relish every second of your exertion, and often they will request further exertions, to make everything "perfect." They may even decide that the result of your exertions were sub-perfect, and then dejectedly act disappointed. Whether it is a big meal you've cooked, a free construction job you did, or some other exertion, not offering to pitch in, or not appreciating the effort is not normal. If I were a woman looking to vet a potential spouse, I would use this information to test whether my future mate was looking for a teammate to join with, in a mutual pursuit, or a slaving abuse sponge, who should shoulder all the misery alone.

Of course the big warning sign is that first narcissistic rage. It is often overlooked, because they hide it for so long at the beginning of the relationship, that by the time they first rage, it will seem out of character, and you will dismiss it as an aberration. The strange thing is, over time, you will become inured to it, and it will not jump out at you as much. They key will be to harness the surprise at that first outburst, realize it may not be an aberration, and begin to look deeper, for more signs of trouble.

195

To look deeper, I would utilize the amygdala hijack, and try to execute various hijacks on a potential spouse. If you can touch their amygdala, and precipitate an uncontrolled rage, you have a pretty good indicator of what kind of a future that relationship will have. Amygdalae will invariably become more sensitive to stimulation as relationships wear on, so if you trigger a rage in a new relationship, that may mean you will be seeing much more rage as that relationship progresses.

Most of all, listen to your gut. Don't offer people the benefit of the doubt, and don't assume some aberrant response is really aberrant. It may be the reality somebody is hiding from you, and the aberrant appearance is just a measure of how diligent they have been in hiding it. When dealing with narcissists, the costs are just too high to not err on the side of caution.

Chapter Twenty-Six

Get a Gun _____

I give this advice to people everywhere, but if you are dealing with a narcissist who poses a threat to your safety, it is especially relevant. I get emails, almost all from women who have gotten away from their narcissist, and who are worried about what their narcissist might do. They are right to be worried. When you have an illogically driven grievance accumulator, who is so panicked by your leaving that they are capable of anything, they could easily become violent. Even worse, by the very nature of their psychology, they won't follow any rules in attacking you. They won't give you a warning, so you can call the cops, and they won't abide by a restraining order issued by a court. They won't even attack you to your face. They will instead, try to hit you when you are most vulnerable, where you are most vulnerable, all when you would never expect it.

If you are afraid of violence from your narcissist, you must understand one thing. You should file police reports, get a restraining order, consult with experts, but in the end, nobody can really help you, if your narcissist decides to do violence. If you want to be safe, you have only one real option - to decide that you will protect yourself. The first part of that process is acclimatizing yourself to the idea of doing violence yourself, in self-defense. You need to run what are called "what-if's."

Those who tactically apply force as a profession, and those who just want to be proficient at it to protect themselves and their loved ones, use as part of their training frequent visualization of incidents that they might encounter. In the visualization of each scenario, they work through how best to handle it. If your town has a rash of car-jackings, you run what-ifs, visualizing how you would handle a car-jacking. If I am sitting at a stoplight, in my car, and a guy tries to carjack me by opening my driver's side door, what would I do? Do I try to draw my firearm immediately, and engage him while still sitting in the seat, and strapped in by the seatbelt? Do I feign unbuckling my belt, and use the movement to cover my draw, to better gain the element of surprise, while still buckled in? Do I feign compliance, unbuckle, and then draw surreptitiously, using my body to keep the perp from seeing my weapon until I am turned in my seat facing him, only letting the perp see my gun as I sweep his gun to the side and unload mine into his chest and face? Execute that last strategy immediately when the threat presents itself, and your chances of success are pretty good. Fumble with uncertainty as you try to figure out what to do on the fly, and you may not do so well.

The what if's serve two purposes. First they help you visualize scenarios, so if they happen, you aren't making up your response as you go along. You have already seen the situation in your head, and if it happens, you already have a good idea of what to do, in what order. A lot of times knowing what you are doing ahead of time, will just make you act faster and more decisively while keeping a cooler head, and acting faster and more decisively, with a clear head, is a huge advantage in such a situation. Know what you are doing, and prepare yourself mentally for every possibility, from tripping and falling, to sustaining an injury, and fighting on through it.

The second effect of visualizing such situations is to acclimatize yourself to the idea of violence. You don't want to be debating in your head if you can kill someone, while in the middle of a lethal encounter. Before you let things get that far, you need to decide, can I kill this person, and if so, then you need to get used to the idea of doing it, and the idea of doing it well, with vigor and zeal.

Hopefully it will never come to it, but if someday you find yourself forced to choose on the spot whether you will live, or whether your narcissist will, you should ideally have made that choice already, and even have a plan ready to apply your decision to the circumstances. Then you should apply that plan forcefully – not just for yourself, but for all your loved ones, and the people whose lives will be ruined by that jackass after he is done ruining yours.

One beneficial side effect of this course of action, is that by developing the ability to protect yourself, you will render yourself and your loved ones safer from all threats, not just this one. In the coming turmoils, being self sufficient, and being able to protect yourself and your loved ones will be a huge advantage.

If you come to the conclusion that you are willing to do violence, as a last resort to save yourself if attacked, and you choose to get a gun, begin by calling a local range, and asking about an NRA Firearms Safety Course. These courses are offered all over the country. They will give you an excellent introduction to firearms and safety procedures, and from there you can ask questions of the experts, and decide on the more complex points, from what gun you wish to purchase, to how to train to use it safely and effectively, to how you intend to keep it available yet secure, to what additional training you want to get, to if you want a carry permit, to how exactly you would use it if pressed.

The bottom line is you are perfectly capable of handing a gun safely, and using it responsibly. I love cops. I have numerous cops in my family, I have known a bunch personally through a variety of venues, and we always get along great. That said, even cops know that they have some real idiots slip through their training, and into their ranks. Even those idiots can be trained and certified to carry a firearm for use in self defense. If they can carry a gun effectively and use it for defense on a daily basis, there is no reason that you, an intelligent, responsible, and kind human being, can not acquire one, keep it safe, and use it to defend yourself once, should the need ever arise.

Don't be ashamed to want to live, and to be willing to take the responsibility into your own hands to protect yourself and your loved ones. Few traits in the world are as noble as the drive to not be a burden through the pursuit of self-sufficiency, and the willingness to protect your own loved ones, no matter the personal cost to yourself.

Chapter Twenty-Seven

The Weirdness _____

I only include this to be as thorough as possible, and to try and help as many people as possible. I don't believe in weirdness. However a lot of people who bump into evil find themselves seeing what appear to be strange things. I had two strange experiences with Bob, myself. Both involved him being enraged, and electrical devices malfunctioning around him. In one case, a circuit breaker in a house blew, timed such that it seemed due to his climaxing anger. In another instance, a car's electrical system malfunctioned, flickering all of the lights erratically, as he grew enraged, only to immediately revert to normal once he left the vehicle and stormed off. I assume both cases were coincidence, but some people who deal with evil do have a tendency to think they see strange things sometimes.

Dr. Scott Peck, the noted psychiatrist, wrote an entire book detailing how two people he dealt with in his psychiatric practice were, in his estimation, actually possessed by demons, who he spoke with during exorcisms. I don't include this to say that this is true, or that the supernatural is behind your narcissist's evil. It probably isn't. But narcissists induce a strange sort of exhaustion in the brain, and you may find yourself thinking you see strange things. It doesn't mean you are going crazy - it may just be a natural part of these types of experiences.

Whether it is supernatural (unlikely), chance (more likely), or just the product of a mind so exhausted by the narcissist, that it has begun seeing things (possibly the most likely of all, given how exhausting these characters can be), you shouldn't become too bothered. Get the narcissist out of your life, and you should be fine, and your problems will be resolved.

I should add an addendum. Decades ago, one relative of Bob's told a story relating to Bob of what sounded like a supernatural occurrence, that they witnessed associated with him, when he was unaware that he was being observed. I didn't really take it seriously. As a result, I didn't pay that much attention to it at the time, and shortly came to forget about it.

Decades later, I was pulled aside by another acquaintance. They proceeded to excitedly recount the exact same, essentially supernatural phenomenon, around Bob, when he was ostensibly unaware that he was being watched. The second witness never knew of the first, at the time they told me the story. Although I trust both witnesses implicitly, I have no idea whether the nature of the mental exhaustion Bob produced could facilitate, purposely or otherwise, an identical hallucination in two different victims, decades apart. Nor can I figure out if it is more or less likely that Bob was in reality a close acquaintance of "his lordship" Beelzebub, who would periodically stop by for a little chat.

I read Scott Peck's book on possession, *Glimpses of the Devil*, wondering if I could read between the lines, and sort out some truth in the matter, but there was none to be had that I could see. From my read, it seemed just as possible his patients (with the heightened amygdala-awareness of narcissists) somehow induced a trance state within him,[1] tricking him into thinking he observed supernatural phenomenon, as it was that he witnessed supernatural phenomenon that weren't recorded on the films of the exorcisms. While I am curious exactly what it was that was going on there, and with Bob, I am just all too happy to see that door closed, mystery or no.

To my knowledge, both witnesses to Bob's anomalies have had no further sightings of the paranormal since leaving his acquaintance. So in my opinion, no matter what you have seen, no matter what mysteries you will leave behind, get the narcissist out of your life, and do it as quickly as you can. There is no problem, even the possibly supernatural, which can't be solved with enough distance between you and them.

---

[1] One of the interesting stories which follows Milton Erickson, the brilliant psychiatrist who is credited as the father of modern hypnosis, is that he could hypnotize his entire class of students, without them ever even knowing that he had put them in a trance. Something about his brain, possibly related to the polio which put him in a coma as a child, had given him an instinctual insight into the brain, which allowed him to exert that kind of control over the brains of others, without their awareness of him exerting such control. It is possible that some narcissists, and the truly evil, due to their grossly aberrant brain function, also have such an innate understanding, and are more capable than we know, within that realm.

Chapter Twenty-Eight

*Separating a Loved One from the Narcissist*___

Perhaps you have armored yourself against the narcissist. You can spot them, repel them, and have ejected all of them from your life. But now, a loved one or friend has become attached to one, perhaps romantically, and you desperately want to spare them the pain which you know is coming.

This is an impossibly difficult situation, in which it pays to first understand what you can and can't accomplish. You can be there for your loved one when things fall apart. You can promise them support if they ever need it, and make good on that pledge. But you cannot explain to the uninitiated the full scope of what the narcissist is, how horrible they are, or how badly they need to get them out of their life. That knowledge can only come from being trapped with a narcissist as their psychological self-control devolves, and they become ever more hysterical, neurotic, and controlling as a result. Until you plumb the depths of that misery firsthand, you cannot really understand it.

Without that knowledge, it is easy to appear to your loved one as if you are the hysteric, grossly overstating the insanity and evil of their partner, who will only be too happy to feed this misperception in an effort to out-group you, and minimize the threat you pose. So first, if possible, I would not be direct or fully honest in any approach of your loved one. You should not, at first, appear adverse to their partner, if at all possible. Do not engage aggressively or start any war, lest you lead your loved one to circle the wagons with their partner, and become more averse to breaking off the relationship, due to the subconscious psychological barriers that they will erect. You can always initiate hostilities later, but for now, you need, more than anything, access to this relationship.

There will be two types of relationships, the new and the old, and each seems to require a different approach.

What you can do if the relationship is new, is try to provoke a devolving of the self-control of your loved one's narcissist, using covertly deployed amygdala hijacks, and similar techniques. The only thing I have found that can split a person (particularly a female) from a narcissist that they are in the infatuation stage with, is the sight of the narcissist grossly losing emotional control in front of others. Let the narcissist lose control ridiculously in front of others, and it can shock your loved one into doing a critical assessment of their relationship. It is that assessment which will open the door to them accepting your input into their mate's fitness.

But for this to be possible you need access, so you must be sure to maintain your relationship with your loved one, and their narcissist. With that access, you will repeatedly walk the narcissist into melting down over inconsequential things, using the covert amygdala hijack. You want them becoming hostile for seemingly no reason, and appearing emotionally dysregulated, in front of your loved one, so they can see the monster within first hand.

This is not something you will do in one sitting, and there will not be a step by step process, that you can be given in a manual. It will require time, to practice pressing different buttons over different insecurities, and seeing what happens. Does the male narcissist have an issue with women having things better than they do? Does he grow irritated at younger individuals getting more attention and accolades than him? Is he overly sensitive to denigrating humor about his accomplishments, competence, or intellect? Political discussions, particularly, can be invaluable in generating emotional engagement and triggering the amygdala.

After each encounter, you need to replay it in your mind again and again. What did he begin to get lit up about? What was the theme you were touching upon? Did you dismiss his opinion? Make fun of his looks? Highlight a failure of his? Talk about one of your friend's ex-boyfriend's amazing abilities? Practice your Hannibal Lector mien as he get's excited, hold intense direct eye contact, make physical contact, such as by squeezing his shoulder, as you emphasize a point likely to set him off. Appear arrogant and amused at his foolishness. Treat him like an overly controlling parent would a child. Invade his space. Scrutinize his expression, and the area around his eyes intensely. Violate his expectations, and laugh uproariously at his unfortunate experiences.

You must make all of your amygdala stimulants appear innocent however. What you want is for him to explode, and for everyone to look, wondering how he could be so crazy as to have melted down emotionally over *that*.

What is most crucial to remember is that if he is a narcissist, and you are right, he is a narcissist because his amygdala can't handle stresses. You can find those sensitive points in his brain, so raw that their presence leaves him emotionally insane, and you can press on them to produce an insane response. If you hit them right, he will not be able to contain himself, and he will reveal his secret.

I would love to say that there is an easier method. *"Explain it to your loved one like this, and they will see the light, and leave immediately."* But when a loved one who is ignorant of the narcissist is in the early, or infatuation stage of a relationship, they are not easily swayed by reason or logic. They will be projecting their own loyalty and decency upon their narcissist. They will excuse minor narcissist outbursts as minor aberrations, that are not really representative of the "real" narcissist's personality. They may perceive your criticism of their narcissist as being critical of their own ability to read people, and dismissive of their own judgment. They may even instinctually circle the wagons with their narcissist, putting you on the outside, and allowing the narcissist to make it ever easier to out-group you, diminish your influence, and eventually split you from the loved one.

If, however, you can trigger an outburst, or any other objectively questionable behavior that makes your loved one notice the defectiveness themselves, while appearing to remain neutral yourself, everything changes. Suddenly, you are not saying that your loved one can't read other people well. You are not criticizing their judgment. Rather, if they have begun to question the narcissist themselves, due to what they have seen, you are affirming their ability to read and judge other people, by telling them that they are right to question the narcissist, and heed their own instincts. Rather than offering weak criticism of a strong opinion they hold, you are strongly fortifying a decision they have already reached themselves. If they have already begun to mentally split from the narcissist, they will also not tend to circle wagons with him, or reject you and your influence. It is a completely different dynamic, and given how difficult the endeavor, one well worth pursuing, regardless of the effort and displeasure involved.

Sometimes you will have a loved one who is in the late stages of a relationship with a narcissist. This is a different dynamic, motivated more by stasis, conditioning, a blind devotion to a concept of loyalty, and the state of being inured to the misery, rather than by the positive euphoria of infatuation mixed with projection of one's own positive traits on the narcissist.

The cases I've observed were all normal females who had endured long periods with male narcissists. I suspect that this is more common than normal males enduring bossy and controlling female narcissists for long periods, due to a difference in psychology between the sexes. Due to a lack of experience with the latter form of this, most of the advice here will relate to the former scenario. If a man is tolerating a female narcissist, there may be a deeper pathology on the man's part, which will make much of the advice here vastly less relevant, and make the situation so difficult as to require a professional's counsel.

In one case I observed, a woman married a narcissist who was astonishingly abusive. Although highly intelligent, educated, and the breadwinner of the family, she seemed to turn off her brain around him, and blind herself to his noxiousness. I suspect it had become like the landscaping outside her house – something she saw in passing every day, but which she never stopped to examine too closely. At maturity, their children wisely fled, going into hiding and refusing to contact them, and eventually she and the narcissist grew old. It seemed as if they would die together, until he went in the hospital one day. While in the bed, he launched into a rage, and she meekly endured it, as always. Afterward, a woman who was with the patient in the other bed in the room pulled her aside, and said sharply, *"You don't have to take abuse like that! There are centers designed to help you."* The woman gave her the phone number for a battered women's helpline, and then left quickly.

She was taken aback, but in a week or so the event had replayed in her mind enough times. She recalled all of the rage she had endured, and tried to understand why this stranger would act as if she was abused. Her thoughts drifted to her children leaving. All at once, she realized what she was enduring was not normal, and she eventually split from her husband.

Another case, briefly mentioned earlier, involved a woman who had been diagnosed with Chronic Fatigue Syndrome, and was almost always confined to her bed. She had a family health emergency, necessitating her return to her parent's home, but her husband could not attend. Within a day or two, her symptoms had fully abated, and she believed she had been miraculously cured. She returned to her husband, and within a day was back in bed, sick and disabled. Thinking it was her house, she and her husband arranged a vacation to the parents home, but she remained sick. They went back home. She eventually went back to her parents alone, and her symptoms again abated. That planted the seed. Eventually they were divorced, and she was permanently cured. Whether he was mildly poisoning her, or it was some psychological effect, I have no idea. The salient point was that it was another case of stasis and conditioning combined with the illusion of mutual devotion, broken only by a shocking realization that the world could have been nice all along.

Another case saw a woman whose husband had to take a week long trip. By the second day, she felt so energized and youthful she reported feeling as if a loving warmth was raining down on her from above, as happiness surrounded her like a cloud of warm fog. Her husband returned, and after a few weeks spent knowing what it was like without him, she promptly arranged another vacation for him. Eventually they divorced, and she reported never being happier.

With these cases in mind, I think the only path you can pursue, if you know such a woman, is to offer her a brief respite from the narcissist. In all three cases, these women didn't know what they were experiencing, until it was removed from their daily lives. Take her on a girl's vacation, get somebody to take her narcissist away for a period, or just find a way to force her to experience a period without the narcissist, so she will realize what she is missing.

In structuring such an intervention, you should understand what the person will go through. Being around a narcissist tends to shut a person's brain off. I have experienced this, and can attest to the fact that it is a powerful effect – so powerful I would never have believed it, had I not experienced it myself. The narcissist is so noxious, that the brain will actually deaden itself neurologically, in preparation for dealing with them, without you even trying to produce the effect – it just happens. The logic the subconscious uses probably runs along the lines of, if the brain is shut off, the noxiousness of the narcissist will be only minimally felt.

The amazing thing is that you will not notice it is shut off, until it turns back on. This shutting off is probably a trainable effect which you develop over time. It is like the proverbial wrestler who picks up a baby calf, and carries it everywhere he goes. Eventually, one day, he is carrying around a cow as if it is nothing, and he has no recollection of ever developing the ability. With the narcissist, one day your brain is turned off, you are barely paying attention to your world, and you have no awareness of this fact.

For many people, it may take as much as two full days of rest, spent without any chance of encountering the narcissist within the next week, for a narcissist-addled brain to come fully back online. When it does, it is an amazing experience. Before this experience, you are in a neurological fog that you are so inured to, you do not even notice it.

After your brain comes back online, you will walk outside, and be hit in the face by warm sunshine. The smell of fresh cut grass and flowers will fill your nose and envelope your being. The colors - of the grass, the trees, the sky, the fluffy clouds, the cars around you, the birds, and everything else, will all jump out at you. The breeze will brush against your face, you will hear bees buzzing and birds singing like never before. And where before you lumbered clumsily, as if wading through molasses while in a trance, your body will move with a snappy energy and forcefulness that you forgot you ever had.

What amazes me is, I was around my narcissist for a total time measured in years. The women described above had been attached for times measured in decades. On my escape, the difference in the quality of my life experience was nothing short of amazing, and yet, I would not be surprised if the women above experienced an even more profound transformation than I did. My description above may be underestimating what those women experienced.

This experience is probably the biggest reason to differentiate between separating someone from a narcissist they have been attached to for a short period, and separating someone who has been in a relationship with a narcissist for a long period. People who have only been attached for a short period will not have seen their brain shut off in the way a long term attachment will produce.

Once someone is in for a long period, you have access to a whole different lever of force, with which to motivate them to split. You simply get them alone, for a week, and turn their brain back on. Once they have smelled that grass, looked up at that neon-royal-blue sky, felt that bright yellow sun rain a deep-penetrating warmth down on their face, and heard all those beautiful birds singing - returning into the cocoon, by re-encountering their narcissist, will not be an option.

You cannot walk out, exhausted, under a cold grayish-blue sky, totally numbed to everything around you, without growing bitter and angry at the narcissist for being so awful. There is not a human alive who could see their brain brought fully online, and then go on to tolerate the deadened-zombie state produced by the noxiousness of the narcissist. Every person you show the real world to will have to leave their narcissist.

I am not sure if you are best off just bringing them to a normal environment, like your home, and letting them experience the nirvana there, or if a tropical vacation is better. A tropical vacation offers the advantage of a lot of stimuli to reignite their brain's activity levels, from reef snorkeling, to palm-lined beaches and the smell of the ocean. However I suspect that it offers the risk that they may associate that nirvana with that place's unique pleasures. If you bring them to a more bland and familiar environment, and they experience the ecstasy, it will be more difficult for them to not realize that their narcissist is their problem.

It would be remiss to not note here that there is a growing field in the manosphere subculture known as "Game" and "Social Dynamics," both of which are dedicated to socially manipulating people, particularly in relationships, using subconscious social cues we are programmed to respond to. The individuals promoting and developing these techniques focus their examination of them primarily on their use in dating and intimate relationships, but their principles apply widely to all areas of social interaction, from work relationships, to family and social structures. If you are interested in other ways to try and free a loved one from the clutches of a narcissist, there will be additional techniques there.[1] However they are the sorts of techniques which require extensive practice and experience to apply, unlike the less technique oriented methods described herein.

Whatever happens, you need to realize that everyone is ultimately responsible for their own lives and happiness. Each of us can only do our best, where we can. If you can free your loved one great. But if you can't, you need to emphasize to them that you will always be there, and then let them come to their own conclusions. Given the noxiousness of narcissists, the conclusion they come to will be inevitable, if given enough time. Be patient.

---

[1]   To begin, stop by Chateau Heartiste <http://heartiste.wordpress.com>. The site could be characterized as risque in places, due to the readership it targets, however the proprietor is brilliant in his presentation of the fundamental ideas behind social dynamics and relationship game. From there, Alpha is Assumed <http://alphaisassumed.wordpress.com> is another excellent site, relaying these concepts in simple, practical form.

Chapter Twenty-Nine

Reactivating Your Own Brain

If you have gotten free of your own narcissist after an extended period in their presence, you may notice that your brain is exhibiting after effects. The problem is that your brain spent a long time being conditioned to look for negativity, and perpetually braced to endure it. A lot of this effect should abate once the narcissist is gone, but some after effects will probably remain. You can't flip a switch and reverse it all immediately, but you can begin to retrain it, by training it to look for, and focus on positivity, and to respond to negativity with action and focus.

With respect to flagging positivity, I am a big fan of vacations. Try to have one regularly, spent in an area which will assail your amygdala with a plethora of positive, stimulating experiences to choose from. Go snorkeling on a reef, or wander through The Baths in the British Virgin Islands. Visit Yosemite National Park. Explore the Bahamas on a chartered sailboat, where you can pet stingrays, feed swimming pigs, ride jet skis, and toss grapes to friendly iguanas – all in the same day.

When you return, remember that sensation, and stimulate it in yourself. Notice the blue sky. Smell the scents in the air on a spring morning. Really taste delicious food, and relish the sensations. Your narcissist may have created a pathway in your brain designed to put you on auto pilot, and you need to overwrite that pathway by repeatedly rewarding your brain with pleasant experiences, in response to it closely looking at the world around you. Eventually, over time, your brain will learn to reflexively look around you to seek out the beauty, so it can enjoy the rewards itself. This will turn your brain back on.

With respect to retraining your brain to engage and deal with negativity, I highly recommend fighting and competition. If you can, join some competitive endeavor. Karate, Boxing, Wrestling, Judo, shooting, or even things like softball, racquetball, soccer, or tennis. You need an activity where you will encounter negativity/challenge, respond with immediate action, and enjoy the camaraderie, and yourself, in the process. Effecting positive changes, such as planting a beautiful landscape, or learning to paint or sculpt, can also train you to take action to ameliorate negativity in the environment, so you can enjoy the subsequent positivity.

Done regularly, all of this will overwrite the bad neural pathways created by the narcissist, replacing them with positive, happy pathways designed to help you focus on the world, enjoy the beauty, and seek out success. In the process you may even acquire a few good friends.

Seeing a professional can obviously also help, so I would recommend you seek that out, if you feel you are not fully enjoying your post-narcissist life as you should. Professionals, with their extensive training, wealth of experience treating different cases, and knowledge of what you experienced can be an invaluable tool. They may be able to offer you a particular way of thinking about things, or of viewing past events, which will allow you to process them much better.

Of course the one thing you should always keep in mind is how much nicer your world is without the narcissist in it. No matter how bad things get, no matter what happens, you now have an experiential baseline by which to measure the good in every future experience. So long as your narcissist is out of your life, things will always be beautiful by comparison.

Chapter Thirty

Conclusion

One of the problems in being normal is that you form emotional attachments, and these will cloud your logical processing. It is normal, and I have done this myself. Even as I ejected Bob from my life, I still projected some measure of humanity upon him, and as a result I felt an emotional need to try and be as nice as possible.

I told myself that he had an affliction, and was damaged in a way which nobody should have to endure. I told myself that he wasn't really responsible for his actions. All of it was malarkey, of course. With the clarifying aspect of temporal distance now between the two of us, I can say he was pure evil – a creature whose sole reason for existence was the misery of everyone and everything around him. He was so evil, that the only way I can really see any logic to his actions is if he was some sort of foot soldier, acting on the orders of a purely evil spiritual entity. Absent that, you are left looking at the wreckage of his life, baffled by how he could so badly need to sabotage his own existence, just to hurt the people whose only sin was being so stupid as to help him, and not expect evil in return.

In your dealing with the narcissist, it will be normal to feel somewhat ambivalent at times, and perhaps even worry about what effect your actions will have upon them. However, you must persevere, and force yourself to do so with ice water in your veins. The narcissist's real advantage is your humanity, and it is what they will use against you. If they succeed, it is what they will point to as the true mark of your stupidity.

Years after everyone cut ties with him, a friend's phone rang and Bob was on the line. He spun a tale of having some sort of cancer, and then proceeded to launch into a sob-story about his dogs, and how he wouldn't be able to keep them. Knowing Bob, the friend remained detached, and waited to see what was coming. As he talked, my friend detected some sort of change periodically in his voice. My friend said it seemed like he was trying, very badly, to fake the natural breaking of one's voice which occurs when one is about to cry, but it was so poorly executed, my friend dismissed the idea that it was some sort of crass attempt at manipulation, and assumed he had a vocal problem, maybe associated with some nerve issue.

Then Bob dropped the bombshell. He was coming to a doctor nearby for testing, and needed a place to crash, so he would be there in a couple of days, and my friend should be ready. My friend declined the opportunity, and Bob proceeded to explode in rage, without any vocal problems whatsoever. A year later, word came back. Bob never had cancer, the testing was a ruse which he forgot about once his attempt to get back in failed, and the whole call was one big attempt at manipulating my friend, based on his emotion and humanity. The friend actually wondered if Bob might have had a plan to try and kill him in the middle of the night, given the ridiculousness of the incident.

Once you get free, you may not have heard the entire end from your narcissist. They know you are human, and as a result, they know you have a weakness. You have humanity, and the full suite of emotional weaknesses which grow from that, from empathy and decency, to loyalty. They will try to exploit all of them. It is important to fully dehumanize your narcissist in your mind, to complete your break from them. If, in your mind, they retain any human qualities, they will use that against you, just as Bob tried to, with my friend.

You are not bending reality when you dehumanize them. The truth is that by ascribing human qualities to them, you are deceiving yourself. I have been amazed as I sank into the depths of Bob's brain, at how hateful and contemptuous he was to everyone – and how much he hid that by feigning normalcy. He didn't view people as human, or even mechanisms – he viewed them as enemies. His outlook was exactly like that of the narcissist who posted on a website to the readers of an article about his own disorder - *"I am a vengeful narcissist and I stick my middle finger to the world and say F#CK YOU ALL. I celebrate myself because I survived YOU.."*

If you are reading this book, it is almost certain that your narcissist is like this. To them, you are a stupid enemy who does what they want, when they press your human buttons – and they resent you even more for forcing them to go to the effort to press those buttons. When they see you miserable, they feel the same relaxation and satisfaction you would feel seeing a child thrive and succeed. When they see you happy, they feel the same painful angst you would feel, seeing a loved one suffer. They are so strange, that they are difficult to imagine.

You can't live with that, and you certainly can't trust it, should it come back around. Dehumanize it, extend it no human courtesy, and repel it at all costs.

I promise, when the dust finally settles, and you have driven them from your life, you will be amazed at the transformation.

I hope this book helps in your battle with your narcissist. Know as you fight, that you are not alone. There are many in the world who have walked in your shoes, who know your plight, and who would give you the shirt off their back, if they thought it could help you. Those who have made the journey before you know that this is a true battle between good and evil, and they want to help good – they want to help you.

After you complete your battle, consider helping someone else somewhere. There are numerous forums online devoted to the narcissist. They can change, so use Google to find the most popular. Find one, and lend your experience to the body of knowledge. Whether you've found a particularly potent amygdala hijack, or you've discovered a way to force the narcissist to think logically, throw it out there so that others may benefit.

If nothing else, helping others will help you to understand what it was you suffered, and how magical the world is, now that you are narcissist-free.

Good luck. And never let yourself forget how beautiful this world is without the narcissist in it.

Further discussion of NPD can be found at the political blog at
http://www.anonymousconservative.com/blog.

www.ingramcontent.com/pod-product-compliance
Lightning Source LLC
Chambersburg PA
CBHW071641280326
41928CB00068B/2153